ODDBALL ILLINOIS

ODDBALL ILLINOIS

A Guide to Some Really

STRANGE PLACES

JEROME POHLEN

CHICAGO
REVIEW
PRESS

Library of Congress Cataloging-in-Publication Data

Pohlen, Jerome.
  Oddball Illinois : a guide to some really strange places / Jerome Pohlen
  p. cm.
  Includes bibliographical references (p. 225).
  ISBN 1-55652-371-8
  1. Illinois—Guidebooks. 2. Illinois—History, Local—Miscellanea. I. Title.
F539.3.P64 2000
917.7304'43—dc21   99-048553

The author has made every effort to secure permissions for all the material in this book.
If any acknowledgment has inadvertently been omitted, please contact the author.

Cover and interior design: Mel Kupfer
Front cover photo: Spindle, sculpture by Dustin Shuler, © 1980
All photographs courtesy of Jerome Pohlen unless otherwise noted.

Published by Chicago Review Press, Incorporated
814 North Franklin Street
Chicago, Illinois 60610
ISBN 978-1-55652-371-7
Printed in the United States of America
10 9 8 7 6 5

TO JIM FROST,
WHO TALKED ME INTO
MY FIRST ROAD TRIP

Contents

INTRODUCTION

Admit it. You secretly love oddballs. Given the choice, you'd rather eat at a diner topped with giant fiberglass weenies than a fast-food outlet. You point out the local haunted cemetery to your impressionable nieces and nephews when they come to visit. And though you spent your last vacation at Disney World, you longed to be watching gator wrestling at the Alligator Safari just down the highway.

The truth is, many people find themselves drawn to oddball attractions, yet seem bound by conventional notions of what constitutes a travel destination. The beach. Yellowstone. The Magnificent Mile. Nobody wants to be the first in the car to say, "Let's stop at the double-decker outhouse!," but doesn't it sound more interesting than Nike Town?

Well, it's time to break out of your shell. *Oddball Illinois* won't tell you the hottest club in Chicago, the quaintest small-town bed and breakfast, nor the most scenic hiking trail in Illinois. You will, however, find the locations of America's One and Only Hippie Memorial, Scarlet O'Hara's green drapes, Popeye's Hometown, and several places the local Chambers of Commerce would just as soon be forgotten.

So if you want to waste your vacation in line behind thousands of other tourists, snapping pictures of places everyone photographs for slide shows nobody wants to see, that's your problem. Don't say you didn't know better. There's more between Chicago and St. Louis than cornfields, and plenty of fascinating places in the Windy City that aren't on Michigan Avenue. Trust me.

While I've made every attempt to give clear directions from major streets and landmarks, you could still become lost on your journey. Don't panic. Think of it as part of the adventure, and remember these tips:

- Stop and ask! For a lot of communities, their Oddball attraction might be their only claim to fame. Locals are often thrilled that you'd drive out of your way to marvel at their underappreciated shrine. But choose your guides wisely; old cranks at the town cafe are good sources, pimply teenage clerks at the 7–11 are not.

- Call ahead. Few Oddball sites keep regular hours, but most will gladly wait around if they know you're coming. This eliminates the infuriating possibility that you'll find yourself standing just outside the World's Largest Collection of Bottle Caps reading a "Gone Fishin'" sign on the door.

- Don't give up. It often happens that your brain starts to shout, "This is stupid!" while you're driving down a country road looking for the World's Largest Bedbug. Perhaps it is stupid, but ask yourself, is it any more stupid than waiting an hour for a table at the Hard Rock Cafe?

- Don't trespass! Once you get to where you're going, don't become a Terrible Tourist. Just because somebody built a sculpture garden in their front yard doesn't mean they're looking for visitors.

Do you have an Oddball site of your own? Have I missed anything? Do you know of an Oddball site that should be included in an updated version? Please write and let me know: Chicago Review Press, 814 N. Franklin St., Chicago, IL 60610.

CHICAGO! CHICAGO!

Chicago has been called many things, so it's odd that it has adopted "The Windy City" and "The Second City" as its nicknames. Both were originally intended as put-downs.

Contrary to popular belief, Chicago is not exceptionally windy. The average wind speed is 10.4 mph, much calmer than in many towns. "The Windy City" is actually a nickname coined by Charles Dana of the *New York Sun*, who was criticizing city boosters as loudmouthed windbags. When Chicago and New York were bidding on the 1893 Columbian Exposition, he advised his readers to "[p]ay no attention to the nonsensical claims of that Windy City. Its people could not hold a World's Fair, even if they won it." Well, they did both, but still the name stuck.

"The Second City" was the title of a derisive piece about Chicago in *The New Yorker* in 1951. It was written by reporter A. J. Liebling, who accused Windy City folk of always wanting to be everything New York already was. Again, rather than take it as an insult, it was adopted by Chicago's citizenry.

These nicknames are much better than titles such as "Hog Butcher Capital of the World" or "Porkopolis," and much preferred to "The Stinky Onion." The name Chicago is a bastardization of Checagou, meaning "wild onion" or "stinky onion," a common plant in the swamps along the river. Early settlers spelled the Native American term "Schuerkaigo," "Shikkago," "Ztschaggo," "Stkachango," and "Psceshaggo," among others, according to Bill Bryson's *Made in America* (1994). Thank goodness they settled on Chicago.

The Loopy Loop
What They Rarely Tell You on the Architecture Tour

Chicago has a lot to be proud of when it comes to architecture. It invented the skyscraper. It has the nation's tallest building. And when Frank Lloyd Wright designed a mile-tall, airplane-blocking super-scraper with atomic-powered elevators, did he propose it be built in New York? Absolutely not! It was Chicago where his massive ego felt at home.

There are some who don't see tall buildings as architectural advancements. They block the light, diminish the humans who live and work in them, and invite a messy form of suicide. Well, the war's over, gang, and the skyscrapers won. Here are a few you should check out on any Chicago visit.

Site of the World's First Skyscraper

Most architectural historians now agree that the 10-story Home Insurance Building, designed by William LeBaron Jenney in 1884 and completed in 1885, was the World's First Skyscraper. A skyscraper is defined as a tall building supported by a steel structure where the exterior walls bear no weight.

Jenney never lived to receive his due, nor did the Home Insurance Building. Its groundbreaking accomplishment was not acknowledged until the building was being torn down in 1931. Historians got a good look at the interior structure as the wrecking ball leveled the innovation floor by floor. Now all there is to look at is a bank.

Home Insurance Building, 135 S. LaSalle, Chicago, IL 60602

Hours: Torn down

Cost: Free

Directions: On the northeast corner of LaSalle and Adams.

Sears Tower

When the Petronas Towers in Malaysia bested the Sears Tower for World's Tallest Building in 1996, architects, many of whom were Americans, started to scramble for broader definitions. They came up with four categories to classify the World's Tallest Building: (1) highest architectural point, (2) highest occupied floor, (3) top of the roof, and (4) top of the antenna. The Sears Tower wins in two of these four categories (2 and 3), and the building's owners were strutting once again.

It is hard not to be impressed by this building. Built in 1973, it's 1,454 feet tall (1,707 if you count the antennas), weighs 222,500 tons, offers 4.5 million square feet of office space (that's 101 acres), and contains enough concrete to build a five-mile, eight-lane highway. If you laid its 43,000 miles of phone lines end to end, it would almost circle the globe twice. Small wonder it has its own zip code: 60606.

The view from the 103rd-floor Skydeck is impressive. You can see four states on a clear day: Illinois, Indiana, Michigan, and Wisconsin. On a foggy day you won't even see Illinois. And on a windy day, you might be able to feel it sway 6–10 inches back and forth, back and forth, back and forth . . .

233 S. Wacker Dr., Chicago, IL 60606

(312) 875-9696

Hours: October–February, daily 9A.M.–10P.M.; March–September, daily 9A.M.–11P.M.

Cost: Adults $8, Seniors(65+) $6, Kids(5–12) $5

www.sears-tower.com

Directions: Bound by Adams, Wacker, Jackson, and Franklin.

Big Car

If you're headed to the Loop, you'll soon discover that most streetside parking is banned. So if you must pay for parking, you should at least support a lot with a sense of humor: the SelfPark on Lake Street.

You could pass it without noticing, so step back and take a good look. The building's facade was designed to look like a 1930s touring car. The floors and railings form a grill and the awnings are two treaded tires. A large vanity license plate says "GOLF," a statue on the roof serves as a hood ornament, and two "headlight" domes finish off the illusion.

SelfPark, 60 E. Lake St., Chicago, IL 60601

(773) 436-7275

Hours: Always visible

Parking hours: Monday–Friday 6A.M.–Midnight, Saturday 7A.M.–Midnight

Cost: Free to view; parking Saturday special $10

Directions: One block east of the El tracks' turn at Lake and Wabash.

E. M. FORSTER
"Chicago—a facade of skyscrapers facing a lake and behind the facade every type of dubiousness."

Tribune Tower

The Chicago Tribune Tower is both a modern gothic masterpiece and the city's greatest monument to institutionalized vandalism. Embedded into the exterior walls of this building are hunks ripped from the world's most famous historic buildings, including the White House, Great Pyramid, Independence Hall, Cologne Cathedral, Westminster Abbey, Fort Sumter, Lincoln's Springfield Home, Notre-Dame-de-Paris, the Alamo, the Parthenon, the Great Wall of China, the Arc de Triomphe, the Kremlin, China's Forbidden City, the Berlin Wall, and the Taj Mahal. Every U.S. state contributed a brick or rock, too. Most are within arm's length, so you can touch these pieces of history if you want.

The Tower contains several unique architectural features. Gargoyles and grotesques on the fourth and fifth floors include an owl with a camera, a monkey, and a porcupine holding a horn. The Robin Hood and howling dog figures over the entryway are the signatures of its architects, Raymond Hood and John Mead Howells.

435 N. Michigan Ave., Chicago, IL 60611

Hours: Always visible

Cost: Free

Directions: Michigan Ave. just north of the Chicago River.

DO NOT take your own samples.

Loop Tour Train

The best and cheapest way to see the downtown architecture is from the elevated railroad tracks of the Loop. But don't take just any El, hop on the Loop Tour Train. Sponsored by the City of Chicago, the CTA, and the Chicago Architecture Foundation, this free narrated ride takes you past some of the city's most famous downtown buildings . . . three times!

The 40-minute tour takes three trips around the elevated loop. On the first time around, volunteer docents tell you the history of public transportation in Chicago and a little about the car in which you are riding. For example, did you know that although each car is designed to accommodate 39 passengers, they have a "crush load" of 150? On the second loop, you'll learn about buildings adjacent to the inside track, and on the final trip they discuss structures off the outside track.

Chicago Office of Tourism Visitor's Center, Chicago Cultural Center, 77 E. Randolph St., Chicago, IL 60602

(312) 744-2400

Hours: May–September, Saturday only, 12:15, 12:55, 1:35, and 2:15p.m.; pick up tickets at 10a.m.

Cost: Free

www.architecture.org/tours_core.html

Directions: Randolph St. at Michigan Ave., docent will lead you to the train station.

YOU SAY IT'S YOUR BIRTHDAY?

For a truly unique experience, stop by the Randolph Cafe on your way out of the Chicago Cultural Center. Every weekday at 1p.m. the City throws a birthday party. Local performers come to celebrate the achievements of a famous individual through songs, readings, and dramatic interpretations. If it's your birthday and you show them a picture ID, you're a guest of honor!

The **311 S. Wacker Building**, otherwise known as the Giant White Castle, is the World's Tallest Reinforced Concrete Structure at 65 stories.

Daniel Goodwin climb the outside of the **Se** **Tower** (233 S. Wacke May 25, 1981, wearir Spiderman costume. trip took 7.5 hours u suction cups.

The former **Conrad Hilton** (720 S. Michigan), site of the 1968 Democratic Convention Riots, used to have an 18-hole golf course atop its roof.

Warren G. Harding was nominated as the Republican candidate for president in the first "smoke-filled room" in American politics. It took place in Suite 804–805 of the **Blackstone Hotel** (636 S. Michigan) on June 11, 1920.

Maude Van Dusen jumped from the **McCormick Building** (332 S. Michigan) on November 25, 1912. A suicide note claimed the Falls City, Nebraska, native and her sister had been forced into prostitution. The tragedy led to the Mann Act (also known as the White Slavery Act) forbidding transport of individuals across state lines for "immoral purposes."

Grant Park was built with rubble from the Chicago Fire. Before the fire, Michigan Avenue bordered Lake Michigan.

A 29-year-old lawyer took off his glasses when chasing a coworker through the **Prudential Building** (138 E. Randolph) in the 1980s. He missed a corner, flew through a window, and fell 39 floors to his death.

The original marble fa**Amoco Building** (200 replaced with granite panels began to buckl is believed to have co building's original cor

The **Hancock Tower** (875 N. Michigan) was supposedly built on the birthplace of Anton LaVey, founder of the Church of Satan. "Spider" Goodwin also scaled this building in November 1981, despite the fire department's attempts to wash him off with buckets and hoses.

n the
adolph) was
he original
replacement
e than the
on.

MORE LOOP BUILDING FACTOIDS

➡ Most Loop buildings are in violation of an obscure 1898 Chicago ordinance that buildings cannot be more than 130 feet tall.

➡ One-third of the world's revolving doors are in Chicago.

➡ According to legend, a ghost's face can be seen peeking out the top windows of Chicago's **Water Tower** (800 N. Michigan), apparently of a man hung from the top in the 1800s. Some witnesses claim to have seen a body hanging from the top. Oscar Wilde once criticized the building: "Your Water Tower is a castellated monstrosity with pepperboxes stuck all over it. . . . It should be torn down."

➡ **The State of Illinois Building** (100 W. Randolph), designed by Helmut Jahn, uses more energy to cool itself in the winter than it takes to heat most buildings. In the summer, the offices near the top have reached temperatures around 115° F.

➡ The **Hancock Tower** (875 N. Michigan) has an 80-foot caged walking deck on the 94th floor where you can feel the high winds without being blown off the roof. (1-888-875-VIEW; 9A.M.–Midnight; Adults $8, Seniors (65+) & Kids(5–17) $6; www.hancock-observatory.com)

➡ The former **Jewelers Building** (35 E. Wacker) once had a parking garage at its center for the first 22 floors. Cars were lifted to their spaces on an elevator.

➡ The netting atop the 27-story **Metropolitan Correctional Center** (71 W. Van Buren) was installed to prevent helicopter escapes after an unsuccessful attempt was made.

➡ **Marina City** (300 N. State) was originally commissioned by the International Union of Janitors to provide affordable housing downtown.

➡ Potter Palmer invited reporters to try and set his "fireproof" hotel rooms afire after the **Palmer House** (17 E. Monroe) was rebuilt in 1871.

➡ There are six different shades of white on the exterior of the **Wrigley Building** (400 & 410 N. Michigan), arranged so that it looks brighter near the top. The bridge between the original building and its annex was built to circumvent state branch banking regulations; there were banks in the ground floors of both buildings and the gangway made them non-branches.

➡ The **Harold Washington Chicago Public Library** (400 S. State) is the World's Largest Public Library with more than two million volumes.

➡ The **First United Methodist Church** (77 W. Washington) is the Tallest Church in the World at 568 feet. It is topped by a Sky Chapel.

➡ The onion dome atop the **Inter-Continental Hotel** (505 N. Michigan) is a holdover from its founding as the Medinah Athletic Club, an offshoot of the Shriners.

➡ Ceres, the Roman goddess of grain, sits atop the **Board of Trade Building** (141 W. Jackson). The 31.5-foot aluminum statue does not have a face.

➡ The **Merchandise Mart** (350 N. Wells) was the nation's largest building until the Pentagon was constructed, and the largest commercial building until the Sears Tower went up. It was purchased in 1945 for its overdue real estate taxes by Joseph Kennedy. The Kennedy family unloaded it in 1998.

➡ **Ludwig Mies van der Rohe**'s first glass-and-steel apartment skyscrapers (860–880 N. Lake Shore Dr.) were built in 1951.

➡ The **Chicago Theater**'s facade (175 N. State) was designed to resemble Paris's Arc de Triomphe.

Eccentric Eateries
Brats, Burgers, Weenies, and More

Chicago isn't known for its *haute cuisine*. Sure, it has its fair share of overpriced, fancy restaurants, but most visitors are looking for deep-dish pizza, cheeseburgers, and Italian beef—blue-collar food for The City That Works. Paris may have given the world vichyssoise and rude waiters, but Chicago has given humankind Twinkies, Cracker Jack, and crock-pots. Would summer barbecues be the same without Chicago-area innovations such as beer cans, screw-cap bottles, and the Weber Grill? And do you know the Kraft General Foods plant (7400 S. Rockwell) makes all the nation's Kool-Aid?

So chuck that Zagat's! Try these eateries with personality.

Hurray for hot dogs!

The Jungle

No discussion of this city's hamburgers and hot dogs would be complete without a little background on Chicago's infamous slaughterhouses.

Chicago's Union Stockyards opened on Christmas Day, 1865. Business expanded until the pens, slaughterhouses, and packing plants covered a square mile bounded roughly by 39th, 47th, Halsted, and Ashland. The Stockyards' operations went relatively unchecked until Upton Sinclair wrote a muckraking exposé in 1906. Though it was a novel, *The Jungle*'s description of life in the yards was nauseatingly accurate. Sinclair hoped it would inspire workers to organize, but its immediate effect was to gross out the reading public, who demanded food and drug reforms. "I aimed at the public's heart, and by accident I hit it in the stomach," he said.

Listen to Sinclair's description of the branch of the Chicago River that ran through the stockyards: "Bubbles of carbolic acid will rise to the surface and burst, and make rings two or three feet wide. Here and there the grease and filth have caked solid, and the creek looks like a bed of lava." Locals called it "Bubbly Creek"; Gustavus Swift was known to inspect the putrid water to make sure his sausage makers weren't throwing out anything usable, and when it comes to sausage, what isn't? It was Swift who first observed, "In Chicago, meatpackers use everything from the pig except the squeal."

The Jungle led to the Pure Food and Drug Act of 1906, but it didn't slow down the yards' operations. An outbreak of hoof-and-mouth disease closed the plants in November 1913, but they quickly reopened. The Union Stockyards reached their operational peak in 1920 when they employed more than 30,000 workers. In that year 300,000 hogs, 75,000 cows, 50,000 sheep, and 5,000 horses were "processed." That's a lot of weenies.

The Union Stockyards finally closed on July 30, 1971. All that remains is a stone entryway, topped by a bull's head, straddling Exchange Avenue. In its 106 years of operation, more than a billion critters met their maker just beyond this gate.

Union Stockyards, 850 W. Exchange St., Chicago, IL 60609

Hours: Always visible

Cost: Free

Directions: Just west of Halsted on Exchange, about 4200 South.

MATTHEW ARNOLD "(Chicago) is a great uninteresting place."

Cheezborger! Cheezborger!

Cheezborgers! No Pepsi. Coke! No fries. Chips! The menu and atmosphere of the Billy Goat Tavern were faithfully spoofed on *Saturday Night Live* by John Belushi and Dan Aykroyd. You'll see not much has changed in 20 years, except that Mike Royko doesn't come around anymore.

The Billy Goat Tavern did not just make an impression on *SNL* cast members and local reporters. It reportedly holds the key to the Cubs' dismal postseason record. The bar's owner, Billy "Goat" Sianis, brought his faithful pet, Billy Goat III, to Wrigley Field during the 1945 World Series. When the pair was ejected, in part because the goat stunk, Sianis put a hex on the Cubs. They quickly blew the series, and Sianis sent the owners a note, "Who stinks now???"

Many years passed before the team returned to postseason play. On July 4, 1983, Sam Sianis tried to get Billy Goat IX into Wrigley Field, but he, too, was rejected by the ushers. Guess what happened to the Cubs? Don't mess with the goat.

Billy Goat Tavern & Grill, 430 N. Lower Michigan Ave., Chicago, IL 60611

(312) 222-1525

Hours: Monday–Thursday 7 A.M.–2 A.M., Friday 7 A.M.–3 A.M., Saturday 10 A.M.–3 A.M., Sunday 11 A.M.–2 A.M.

Cost: Meals $2–$5

Directions: Below the Wrigley Building, just north of the Chicago River.

EAT UP!

Sometimes it isn't just four-legged animals that end up in sausage casings. On May 1, 1897, Louisa Leutgert disappeared. Her husband Adolph was a noted local sausage baron with a violent temper and a full-time mistress. Police searched Leutgert's factory and found suspicious evidence in one of the large vats: teeth, a bone from a big toe, and Mrs. Leutgert's wedding ring engraved with "L.L." Adolph was charged with Louisa's murder and eventually convicted after a second trial. Though the vat was supposedly being "cleaned" with potash at the time of the murder, wiener sales plummeted that summer. Louisa's ghost was said to haunt Adolph the rest of his days. The sausage factory (Hermitage & Diversey) burned down in 1902.

The Chicago Shrine

Tucked under the Red Line El tracks at the Fullerton stop is a tiny hotdog joint that honors Chicago. Not Chicago, the city; Chicago, the *band*. Hard to believe, but someone has immortalized this prom-song factory. Owner Peter Schivarelli was pushing hot dogs when he decided to become the local band's never-go-away kid brother. He would eventually become part of its management.

Schivarelli saved many of Chicago's gold records, musical instruments, and concert posters. They now plaster the walls of his weenie stand. He also has a collection of autographed pictures from the likes of Jessica Hahn, Jimmy Buffet, Jeremy Jordan (remember him?), and Ara Parsegian. Their Vienna Dogs are great, but you have to endure an endless-loop tape of Chicago's songs blaring over the sound system.

Demon Dogs, 944 W. Fullerton Ave., Chicago, IL 60614

(773) 281-2001

Hours: Monday–Friday 6A.M.–10P.M., Saturday–Sunday 8A.M.–8P.M.

Cost: Meals $2–$5

www.chirecords.com

Directions: Under the El tracks, east of Southport.

Blue Frog Bar and Grill

River North is awash in Hard Rock and Rainforest Cafes: long lines, over-priced food, and attached gift shops. Who needs them? If you're looking for a place with style in this canned-restaurant Hell Zone, stop by the Blue Frog Bar and Grill.

The proprietors came up with this game-themed joint over a bottle of Jose Cuervo in 1988. Rock-'em, Sock-'em Robots and game boxes dangle from the ceiling, and dozens of well-worn board games are crammed into cubbyholes along the walls. Feel free to bring them to your table! Nobody will hassle you to buy a Blue Frog T-shirt. The longer you play, the longer you eat and drink. They've got the classics, like Monopoly and Battleship, but they've also got oldies, like the Vince Lombardi Game and the Patty Duke Game. Then they have ones you've never heard of, such as Ginnykub and Conspiracy. Twister is better after you've had a few. Warning: Don't start playing Risk too close to closing time because they will not keep the joint open until you conquer the world; one group had to leave a $20 deposit so they could continue after hours in the parking lot, then returned the game the next day.

The Blue Frog serves a broad menu of Mexican food and burgers, and the service is fast. You'll be able to finish your dinner and a game of Scrabble before your friends get a table at Michael Jordan's Restaurant, so order another round and shuffle those tiles.

676 N. LaSalle, Chicago, IL 60610

(312) 943-8900

Hours: Monday–Friday 11:30A.M.–Midnight, Saturday 8P.M.–3A.M.

Cost: Lunch $5–$10

Directions: At the corner of LaSalle and Huron.

The Matchbox

If you want any elbow room at The Matchbox, you should apply for a job, because there is more room behind this bar than there is in front of it. This sliver of a drinking establishment is widest at the front door, about two stools worth, and tapers to a point at the rear. When you sit at the bar your back is nearly resting on the front window. This makes for cozy drinking. Be sure you're sitting next to the person you want to speak to, because you'll be beside them all evening.

The Matchbox is best known for its vodka gimlets: lime juice and egg whites served in a martini glass, its rim ringed with powdered sugar. High in vitamin C, low in cholesterol, and it almost glows in the dark. What could be better for you?

770 N. Milwaukee Ave., Chicago, IL 60622

(312) 666-9292

Hours: Roughly 4P.M.–2A.M.

Cost: Gimlets $4

Directions: At the corner of Ogden Blvd. and Milwaukee Ave.

CHICAGO CULINARY CREATIONS

So your idea of eating out is parking after you drive thru instead of taking it home. Well then, Chicago is your kind of place. Fast food, fattening food, all created right here in the City of Big Shoulders and Stomachs. *(continued next page)*

➡ **Beer Cans** In 1935 Chicago's American Can Company introduced its post-Prohibition sensation to a thirsty nation.

➡ **Cracker Jacks** F. W. Rueckheim first sold Cracker Jacks at the 1893 Chicago World's Fair; prizes weren't included until 1913. Cracker Jack, the boy, was fashioned after his grandson, Robert. Today the snack food is manufactured in suburban Northbrook.

➡ **Crock-Pots** The 1970s sensations were invented by Rogers Park engineer Irving Naxon. The crock-pot was originally named the "Naxon Beanery."

➡ **Deep-Dish Pizza** Known around the world as Chicago-style pizza, the first deep-dish was served at Pizzeria Uno (29 E. Ohio) in the 1940s. It was the invention of Ric Riccardo and Ike Sewell.

➡ **Dove Bars** The first Dove Bars were produced in 1952 by Leo Stefanos at his South Side confectionery (61st & Pulaski).

➡ **Foot-Long Hot Dogs** Riverview Amusement Park (Belmont & Western) began selling foot-longs in the 1930s.

➡ **Screw-Cap Bottles** Edward Ravenscroft of Abbott Laboratories in North Chicago (Waukegan Rd.) patented the screw-cap bottle in 1936.

➡ **Sundaes** Deacon Garwood invented the sundae after Evanston banned seltzer water on the Sabbath. Ice cream and syrup were legal. The name's modified spelling reflects Evanston's blue laws.

➡ **Twinkies** The manager of the Continental Baking Company's Hostess Bakery in Schiller Park, James Dewar, concocted the snack food in 1930. Dewar claimed he ate two Twinkies every day for the rest of his life, and lived into his eighties.

➡ **Weber Grills** Mount Prospect metal worker George Stevens made the first Weber Grill (also known as George's Bar-B-Q Kettle) in 1951 at the Weber Brothers Metal Works of Palatine, his employer.

Mini-Museums
Shoebox Showcases

It's not hard to find the Art Institute. As a vacation stop, it's not very original either. Why not visit some of Chicago's lesser-known, but equally fascinating, museums? This city has specialized collections dedicated to the human foot, holography, radio, and surgery. Surely one of those topics might interest or intrigue you.

Feet First

Who would have thought the human foot was so interesting? Dr. Scholl, that's who!

William Scholl began his career as a shoemaker, but in 1904 branched out into products for shoe injuries: bunion pads, callous protectors, corn pads, and sole inserts. They were a welcome offering to the foot-weary public and made Dr. Scholl a household name.

You'll learn all about the history of footwear and footcare at Feet First, a museum on the ground floor of the Scholl College of Podiatric Medicine. As you walk through the lobby you'll see historical footwear from an era before left and right shoes were common. Even after form-fitting, arch-supporting shoes became the norm, modern shoes had problems. Read the warnings: "In the 1970s, these platform shoes were stylish, but the wearer risked falling because of their height and inflexibility."

Feet First has many hands-on, er, feets-on exhibits. Step on the Meet Your Feet pressure pads and learn why your dogs get so tired. Rest your tootsies in the EZ Your Feet Theater as you watch Scholl's life story. His credo? "Early to bed, early to rise, work like hell, and advertise." And check out foot-related oddities, like the fluoroscope, an X-ray device for measuring feet in the 1950s, and the oversized shoes worn by professional basketball players.

1001 N. Dearborn, Chicago, IL 60610

(312) 280-2487

Hours: Monday–Tuesday, Friday 9A.M.–4P.M., Wednesday–Thursday 9A.M.–7P.M.

Cost: Free

www.bigfoot.scholl.edu/e/index.htm

Directions: Three blocks north of Chicago Ave., adjacent to Washington Square Park.

> **JOHN GUNTHER** "Chicago is as full of crooks as a saw with teeth."

Enough with the "woody" jokes.
Photo by author,
courtesy of Museum of
Broadcast Communications

Museum of Broadcast Communications and Electronic Media and Radio Hall of Fame

This museum celebrates America's obsessions with both TV and radio, though the emphasis is on the latter. Whether you're a vidiot or a radiot, there's something here for you.

The Radio Hall of Fame tries to put a visual face on a nonvisual medium. You'll see Fibber McGee's junk-filled closet, Jack Benny's vault, and Edgar Bergen's Charlie McCarthy, Mortimer Snerd, and Effie Klinker puppets. A small, working radio studio adjoins the museum where you can sometimes sit in on a live radio show.

In the Television Exhibit Gallery you'll find a camera used to broadcast the first Kennedy-Nixon debate and the puppet Garfield Goose. Try your skills at newscasting in a simulated studio with a simulated script, just like simulated journalists, also known as news anchors. Down the hall, visit the Advertising Hall of Fame and watch endless hours of program-free commercials. They only play the best ads, so you won't be wasting your time.

But the best part of the MBC is its 70,000+ episode collection of American radio and television shows. If you'd like to track down a childhood memory, or just that episode where Mork battles Fonzie, they can help you out. The service is open to the public for a minimal fee.

78 E. Washington St., Chicago, IL 60602-3407

(312) 629-6000

Hours: Monday–Saturday 10A.M.–4:30P.M., Sunday Noon–5P.M.

Cost: Free; viewing carrels $2

Directions: At Michigan Ave. and Washington.

International Museum of Surgical Sciences and Hall of Immortals

Everybody's a collector, even surgeons, especially Dr. Max Thorek. The instruments and artifacts he collected served as the seed for this museum's galleries. Over the years, other surgeons also sent their most prized finds to this place, expanding it to a 7,000-piece exhibit, including

- a copy of Napoleon's death mask
- a bronze speculum found in Pompeii
- Florence Nightingale's nurse's cap
- a Chippendale wheelchair
- a working iron lung from the 1920s
- trepanned (drilled) Peruvian skulls
- ancient stone circumcision knives
- amputation kits and artificial limbs
- Aztec charms
- one of the world's first stethoscopes
- a full-sized apothecary shop
- the Adrian X-ray Shoe Fitter

and much, much more!

The most surprising part of this collection is not the instruments, but the art. You can find a rendering of the first ovarirectomy, with doctors removing a basketball-sized tumor, Dr. Dorry Pasha operating on a case of elephantiasis of the scrotum, a geisha having her arm removed by Dr. Pompe V. Meerdervoort, and Xavier Cugat's painting of an operating room where a surgeon reads a *Playboy* and a dog waits for scraps. And they've got dozens of busts of famous surgeons, many carved by other doctors, demonstrating that you can be handy with a scalpel and not with a chisel.

If you can't make it to the museum, visit their Web site, where you will contract an "Antique Illness" and hopefully be cured. One drawback: you can only use antique remedies. Little wonder there are more dead visitors than live ones.

1524 N. Lake Shore Dr. Chicago, IL 60610-1607

(312) 642-6502

Hours: Tuesday–Saturday 10A.M.–4P.M.

Cost: Adults $5, Seniors $3, Kids $3

www.imss.org

Directions: One block south of North Ave. on inner Lake Shore Dr.

They call him Uncle Fun for a reason.

Uncle Fun

While technically not a museum, Uncle Fun sure feels like it, and the best part about it is you can buy the exhibits! They've got spider rings and Scooby Doo magnets, snow globes and windup toys, rubber rats and 1950s postcards, costume jewelry and 3-D Jesus portraits . . . thousands of pop-culture doodads tucked in old card catalogs, crammed in bins, or piled on the counter. If you don't know what you want, you'll *still* find it at Uncle Fun's.

Ted Frankel, also known as Uncle Fun, has been in the ephemera business for more than two decades in what he describes as "a habit that got out of control." He insists that his clientele is strictly kids, though he admits that some come in older bodies. Ted scours the country looking for toy closeouts and mass market knickknacks, always keeping three criteria in mind: (1) the item must be visually exciting, (2) it must be cheap, and (3) it must be fun. Talk about a dream job!

Three times a year, Uncle Fun holds fabulous garage sales. Get the dates and mark them on your calendar; they are not to be missed. Closeouts and overstocks, slightly dented and mint condition, it's spring cleaning at the coolest toy chest in town.

1338 W. Belmont, Chicago, IL 60657

(773) 477-8223

Hours: Monday–Saturday Noon–7P.M., Sunday Noon–6P.M.

Cost: Free; toys extra, but not much

Directions: Two blocks east of Ashland on Belmont.

Museum of Holography

This small but impressive museum is the only one in America dedicated to the science and art of holography. While there is some attempt to explain how the images are produced, it's mostly a showcase for holographers' works. Large, painting-sized pieces hang in a darkened gallery for easy viewing. Watch Michael Jordan pass a basketball behind his back. Check out the Laser Lady, a Nancy Sinatra look-alike in go-go boots. Two of the best pieces are the "Fortune Teller" and "Aquarius," though "Eddie Smooching" will melt your heart. Eddie's an orangutan.

A separate gallery is reserved for voxgrams, three-dimensional images made from clinical data. Human organs are rendered in space, such as kidneys and testes, so doctors don't have to get their hands all icky. If you'd like to purchase a 3-D picture of your own, there's a gift shop, too.

1134 W. Washington Blvd., Chicago, IL 60607

(312) 226-1007

E-mail: hologram@flasj.net

Hours: Wednesday–Sunday 12:30P.M.–5P.M.

Cost: Adults $2.50

www.museumofholography.com

Directions: Just east of Racine on Washington Blvd.

Public Art
Little-Known Masterpieces in Fiberglass, Concrete, and Bronze

Formal, public art in Chicago is confusing. There's a statue of Abraham Lincoln in Grant Park, and a statue of Ulysses S. Grant in Lincoln Park. Were their work orders mixed up? And what about Claes Oldenburg's *Batcolumn* outside the Harold Washington Social Security Center (600 W. Madison)? It has nothing to do with Batman; it's a 101-foot baseball bat. Kind of ironic for a city with two baseball teams, one known for throwing the World Series and the other for being a perpetual loser. And who knows what that Picasso in Daley Plaza (50 W. Washington) is? A baboon? A woman? A lion?

While everyone's deeply confused about the high-brow, subsidized art of the city, nobody's paying any attention to the commercial creations, the fiberglass masterpieces, the downright odd and misplaced public art pieces of Chicago. Nobody, that is, but this travel guide.

Big Ball and Pin

The Woodmac Lanes may be out of business, but its giant bowling ball and pin still loom over Western Avenue, ready to pick up that 7–10 split. The pin had BOWL outlined in neon and the ball urged passersby to stop by their snack bar for cocktails. It must have been a classy joint.

Woodmac Lanes, 7601 S. Western Ave., Chicago, IL 60620
Hours: Always visible; bowling alley is closed
Cost: Free

Mussolini's Pillar

You might think it insensitive to have a public monument, donated by a Fascist dictator who cost thousands of American veterans their lives, in the shadow of Soldier Field . . . and you'd be right . . . but there it sits: the Balbo Monument, also known as the Mussolini Pillar.

The Balbo Monument was dedicated in 1933 at the Century of Progress Exposition. The 2,000-year-old Roman column sits atop a pedestal that reads, "Fascist Italy, with the sponsorship of Benito Mussolini, presents to Chicago a symbol and memorial in honor of the Atlantic Squadron, led by Balbo, which with Roman daring, flew across the ocean in the 11th year of the Fascist Era."

Balbo was shot down by his own troops during WWII, Mussolini was hung by his heels by his countrymen, but the pillar remains, as does the Grant Park boulevard named for the Italian flying ace.

Burnam Park, 1550 S. Lake Shore Dr., Chicago, IL 60605
Hours: Always visible
Cost: Free
Directions: Between Soldier Field and McCormick Place, along the Burnham Harbor bike path.

Big Weenies

The Big Weenies atop the Superdawg Drive-In are Chicago's best-known commercial statues, and for good reason. The Tarzan Weenie is clad in a leopard skin and strikes a muscleman pose, while the topless Jane Weenie wears a miniskirt and looks on adoringly. (Cut them some slack on the sexist imagery; these were built in 1948.) Both have glowing eyes that are best appreciated after dark.

Superdawg is owned by Maurie Berman, and it is one of the last great drive-ins. You never have to leave your car; just place your order through the call boxes and the carhops will bring the food. The burgers are awesome, the service is better, and the weenies are enormous.

Superdawg Drive-In, 6363 N. Milwaukee Ave., Chicago, IL 60646
(773) 763-0660
Hours: Always visible
Store Hours: Sunday–Thursday 11A.M.–1A.M., Friday–Saturday 11A.M.–2A.M.
Cost: Meals $3–$6
Directions: At the intersection of Milwaukee, Devon, and Nagle.

It's SUPERDAWG!

Halt! For a great offer on contacts . . .

Eye Care Indian

Perched atop the Capitol Cigar Store on the South Side is a two-story Indian. His arm is upraised in a gesture of "Howdy!" or "Halt!," depending on your point of view. To avoid the negative association between cigar stores and Indian statues, a sign for an Eye Care Center has been hung around his neck. That ought to silence the critics!

Capitol Cigar Stores International, 6258 S. Pulaski Rd., Chicago, IL 60629

(773) 582-5776

Hours: Always visible

Store Hours: Monday–Saturday 9:30A.M.–6:30P.M.

Cost: Free

Directions: At the intersection of 63rd and Pulaski.

Faces on the Wall

One of the strangest murals in the Pilsen area is a collection of faces beneath the railroad tracks that form the community's northern boundary. It was created by the 1997 Summer Program in the Arts and features dozens of detailed, three-dimensional faces jutting out from the cement abutment. Their eyes are all closed so they appear deceased, like Mob hits encased in cement. To brighten up the image some, bodies have been painted around the faces.

Pilsen is filled with many stunning murals. Some are decades old, and others are still wet when you see them. The best old murals are on 16th Street, along the tracks. They cover a wide variety of topics, from Che Guevara to Speedy Gonzalez. The community's more modern murals can be seen along Ashland Avenue.

1500 S. Blue Island Ave., Chicago, IL 60608

Hours: Sunrise–sunset

Cost: Free

Directions: On the east side of Blue Island as it passes under the railroad tracks.

Bundy Fountain Light Show

Though its history is refined, the Buckingham Memorial Fountain is best known as the opening shot on *Married with Children*. In fact, many European visitors are surprised to learn that its name isn't the Bundy Fountain.

The Buckingham Fountain is based on a fountain at Versailles and is named after Clarence Buckingham, brother of Kate Buckingham, its funder. It pumps 14,000 gallons a minute, some of it 200 feet into the air. Every night during the summer there's a Light Show. It's well worth the trip downtown, unless Grant Part is overrun by Taste of Chicago or Blues Fest revelers.

Buckingham Fountain in Grant Park, 100 N. Lake Shore Dr., Chicago, IL 60601

(312) 747-2200

Hours: Summers; Light Show 9–10P.M.

Cost: Free

Directions: Where Congress meets Columbus.

NELSON ALGREN
"Loving Chicago is like loving a woman with a broken nose."

Hamburger Man

He's huge. He's happy. He's Hamburger Man! Sharing a rooftop with a giant blushing hot dog, Hamburger Man is far more outgoing. Drivers headed south on Milwaukee Avenue are greeted by his friendly, fiberglass wave. Students at Schurz High School across the street are protected by his benevolent presence. And Hamburger Man doesn't even seem to mind that he is in sorry need of a paint job. What a trooper!

Pig Out Hot Dogs, 3591 N. Milwaukee Ave., Chicago, IL 60641

(773) 282-1200

Hours: Always visible

Store Hours: Monday–Friday 10:30A.M.–3P.M.

Cost: Free

Directions: At the intersection of Milwaukee and Addison.

Radium Gals

This event happened at a factory along the Illinois and Michigan Canal years ago. Women painting glow-in-the-dark clock faces were told to lick their brushes between applications to keep the tips pointy. Unfortunately, the glowing paint contained radium and most of the women came down with cancer.

The whole sordid affair is commemorated as part of the large mosaic bench at Gateway Park at Navy Pier. Scenes from the canal's history are laid out in tile, and the Radium Gals' poisoning is just one panel. Look for the woman painting an alarm clock.

Navy Pier, 600 E. Grand Ave., Chicago, IL 60611

(312) 595-PIER

Hours: Daily 8A.M.–10P.M.

Cost: Free

www.navypier.com

Directions: East of North Pier, on the first bench facing away from the pier.

Birth of the Bomb

By far the strangest piece of formal sculpture in Chicago is a piece that marks a turning point in the 20th Century: the birth of the Bomb. Henry Moore's 1967 sculpture, called *Nuclear Energy*, sits on the exact spot where the first nuclear reaction took place on December 2, 1942.

At the time, Enrico Fermi's lab was in a squash court under the west grandstand of Stagg Field. Thrilled as his team was at their accomplishment, it was revealed years later that the crew wasn't entirely sure that the chain reaction would stop once started. Perhaps that's why they were so happy.

Stagg Field was torn down years ago due to, among other problems, radiation contamination. (A new Stagg Field has been erected a few blocks away.) Much of the stadium rubble was trucked out to Palos Hills and buried in Red Gate Woods, along with other "hot" waste from the Manhattan Project. Signs at the woods read, "Caution, do not dig. Buried in this area is Radioactive Material."

Some say Moore's work looks like a human skull. Others say it resembles a modified mushroom cloud. But no matter which way you look at it, it's not encouraging.

Nuclear Energy Statue, 5651 S. Ellis St., Chicago, IL 60637

Hours: Always visible

Cost: Free

hep.uchicago.edu

Directions: On the east side of Ellis between 56th and 57th Sts.

Radioactive Waste Dump, Red Gate Woods, Palos Hills, IL 60465

Hours: Daily 7A.M.–10P.M.

Cost: Free

Directions: Near Archer Ave. and 107th St.

Other People's Stuff
Why Is This Stuff in the Windy City?

OK, so you're being forced to go to the Big Museums. None of your friends would forgive you if you came home without a Sue the Dinosaur T-shirt or a *Sunday Afternoon on the Island of La Grande Jatte* canvas tote bag. Use your visit to explore and uncover the weirdness within these hallowed institutions. Skin from the snake in the Garden of Eden? Man-eating lions? The first telescope to see Uranus? They're all there if you look hard enough.

Chicago Historical Society

The Chicago Historical Society is a prime example of a museum that seems to have a wealth of exhibits that belong somewhere else. You'd expect artifacts from the Chicago Fire, but why is George Washington's inaugural suit here? Thankfully, the museum isn't shy about mixing these incongruous items in among its genuine Chicago stuff, nor do they avoid displaying less pleasant aspects of the city's past, like a stuffed ballot box or a foot-long cleaver used to kill cattle at the stockyards before electric saws were invented. Artifacts rotate, so some of their goodies might be in storage when you visit, but here's just a sampling of what you might find:

- Lincoln's Death Bed. Abe had to be laid out diagonally because he was too long.
- Mary Todd Lincoln's bloody Ford's Theater cape.
- Dillinger's 1934 death mask, taken at the Cook County Morgue.
- Chief Black Hawk's death mask.
- Jane Byrne's inauguration ensemble.
- Al Capone's official 1931 mug shot.
- Melted spoons, plates, bottles, and marbles from the Chicago Fire.
- John Brown's Bible with all the fire and brimstone passages underlined.
- "Any holder but a slave holder" embroidered pot holders.
- The Emancipation Proclamation table from the White House.
- Robert E. Lee's Appomattox Surrender table.
- Two unexploded pipe bombs reportedly found near Haymarket Square after the riot.
- Hugh Hefner's pajamas and smoking pipe.
- Stripper Sally Rand's seven-pound fans used during her Paramount Club act (16 E. Huron).
- TV puppets Kukla and Ollie.
- Michael Jordan's 1989 uniform, including Nike shoes.
- George Washington's second inaugural suit, spyglass, and compass.
- The *Chicago Tribune*'s "Dewey Defeats Truman" blunder issue.

Some of the things you won't see include an early draft of the Emancipation Proclamation (which was destroyed along with the first Chicago Historical Society during the Chicago Fire) and bone chips from the 12 Apostles (which the museum auctioned off).

1601 N. Clark, Chicago, IL 60614-6099

(312) 642-4600

Hours: Monday–Saturday 9:30A.M.–4:30P.M., Sunday Noon–5P.M.

Cost: Adults $3, Seniors(65+) $2, Kids(6–17) $1, Mondays free

www.chicagohs.org

Directions: At the south end of Lincoln Park at Clark St. and North Ave.

Parakeets on the Loose

If you find the Lincoln Park Zoo overwhelming, or are philosophically opposed to the caging of animals, perhaps you should visit Hyde Park, where critters roam free. Not just any critters: monk parakeets! Sometimes known as quaker parrots, these Brazilian natives escaped from a pet shop truck in the 1970s and established their nests on the power poles and trees of Hyde Park.

They've survived the city's bitter winters, death squads from the U.S. Fish and Wildlife Service, and crews from Commonwealth Edison. If the parakeets had an ally it was the late Mayor Harold Washington. Several nests were located just behind his apartment building, and Washington saw in them the same determination he needed to run the city. Now he's gone, but the birds are still there.

The monk parakeets are not difficult to locate. They build enormous, crazy nests of large twigs, are bright green, and squawk loudly. Stand on the corner of 53rd and Shore and listen; they're bound to call you over.

GEMS OF THE OTHER BIG MUSEUMS

Saltwater, Shedd Aquarium (1200 S. Lake Shore Dr., (312) 939-2438, www.shedd.org) That's not just any saltwater in those tanks! It was shipped in 160 boxcars from Key West in 1930.

***American Gothic* by Grant Wood**, Art Institute of Chicago (111 S. Michigan, (312) 443-3600, www.widow.artic.edu/aic) The painting provides a great opportunity for a gag photo, but it's very difficult to sneak a pitchfork past the Art Institute guards.

The Uranus Telescope, Adler Planetarium (1300 S. Lake Shore Dr., (312) 922–STAR, www.adlerplanetarium.org) William Herschel used this Uranus Telescope, housed in the world's first planetarium, to spot the distant planet in 1781.

Hyde Park, 1650 E. 53rd St., Chicago, IL 60637

Hours: Sunrise–sunset

Cost: Free

Directions: 53rd St. at Shore Drive near Eastview Park, just west of Lake Shore Dr.

Many, Many Mummies

The Oriental Institute is a brave institution. Ignoring the possible consequences of ancient curses, they've dragged out a huge collection of
Egyptian mummies for all to see. And not just human mummies, but
preserved hawks, crocodiles, rodents, and ibises. You name it, the
Egyptians wrapped it.

The museum has been undergoing extensive renovations and will
not be fully operational for several years. But for the time being, the
Egyptian Gallery is open. In addition to the mummies, they've got hundreds of statues, jugs, scarabs, and dioramas of the pyramids.

Oriental Institute, 1155 E. 58th St., Chicago, IL 60637

(773) 702-9521

E-mail: oi-museum@uchicago.edu

Hours: Tuesday, Thursday–Saturday 10A.M.–4P.M., Wednesday 10A.M.–8:30P.M., Sunday
Noon–4P.M.

Cost: Free

www-oi.uchicago.edu

Directions: Just east of Woodlawn on 58th St., on the campus of the University of Chicago.

Ziggy, Bushman, Sue, and the Man-Eaters

The stuffed critters at the Field Museum are a sordid lot. If you look
into their glassy eyes today they appear docile and lovable, but things
were different when human-hating blood flowed through their veins.

Take Ziggy the Elephant. He started life with Singer's Midget
Circus, smoking cigarettes and playing the harmonica to everyone's
delight. But in 1941 he killed a marine band trombonist in San Diego's
Balboa Park. This landed him in solitary at the Brookfield Zoo, where
he nearly gored his trainer, George "Slim" Lewis, and tossed turds at
unsuspecting schoolchildren. Ziggy died in his cage in 1975 and his
bones were boiled down for the Field to display.

And then there's Bushman, the much-loved gorilla from the
Lincoln Park Zoo. He arrived in Chicago in 1930 and over the next 20

years chucked his fair share of excrement. He also assaulted a few visitors who got too close to his cage. Bushman died on January 1, 1951, and while Chicago mourned, he was stuffed for Field patrons.

Sue, the most famous *T. rex* fossil ever unearthed, never killed a human, but she did cost Walt Disney and McDonald's $8.36 million. That's a lot of Happy Meals and *Lion King* videos, so believe me, somebody will suffer. Sue was named for Sue Hendrickson, the South Dakota paleontologist who discovered her in 1990. Sue's reconstructed skeleton will be unveiled in 2000 at both the Field Museum and Dinoland in Orlando. Two Sues? Yes, one's either a Disney miracle or a clever reproduction.

But the hands-down winners in the Field's human-hurting collection are the Lions of Tsavo, two big cats believed to have devoured more than 130 railway workers in East Africa in 1898. Their story, and the story of the man who shot them, was made into the movie *The Ghost and the Darkness*. These male lions are odd in that they do not have manes. They were felled by John Patterson, a civil engineer on the railroad, and were purchased by the Field Museum in the 1920s.

Field Museum of Natural History, Lake Shore Dr. and Roosevelt Rd., Chicago, IL 60605
(312) 922-9410
Hours: Daily 9 A.M.–5 P.M.
Cost: Adults $4, Kids $2.50, Thursdays free
www.fmnh.org
Directions: On the south end of Grant Park, east of the Loop.

Happy Homes and Bizarre Businesses
Living Well (and Weird)

According to the Commission on Chicago Landmarks, there are 12 "popular" house types in the city. That's it. Twelve. Chicago Cottages, Frame Houses, Queen Annes, Graystones, Stone Rows, Brick Rows, Apartment Buildings, Two- and Three-Flats, Storefronts with Apartments, Prairie Schools, Bungalows, and Suburban-Style Chicago Houses. Three million people in *12* different houses?

Well, not exactly. There are a few who step outside the mainstream. Take, for example, the old Palmer Mansion. Socialites Bertha and Potter Palmer built a garish castle at 1350 N. Lake Shore Drive in 1882, and to ensure that they never had to receive any uninvited or out-of-favor guests, none of the entrances had external doorknobs. If you wanted in, a servant had to open the door from inside.

The Castle was razed in 1950 to make way for an even more hideous high-rise, so there's nothing left to admire. But there are several unique structures in the Windy City worth taking a look at. They may not be "popular," but they are cool.

Ship-Shaped Beach House

A daydreaming tourist driving down Lake Shore Drive might think a steamer ship has run aground near North Avenue. But it turns out to be nothing more than a ship-shaped concession stand, lifeguard station, and restroom facility.

The original North Avenue Beach House was constructed in 1938 by WPA workers. Though made of little more than plywood, it lasted until 1998–99 when another beach house was erected. The new structure is even more realistic than its predecessor and includes two smokestacks, a mast, and two fake air vents on the roof/deck.

North Avenue Beach House, 1700 N. Lake Shore Dr., Chicago, IL 60610

Hours: Always visible

Cost: Free

Directions: North Ave. Exit from Lake Shore Dr.

Mr. Imagination's Grotto

Greg Warmack is one of Chicago's best known intuitive artists, but few people know him by his real name. Instead, they call him Mr. Imagination.

Mr. Imagination has been creating art from discarded objects for years. He is famous for using bottle caps to build thrones, crowns, and walking sticks, but he turned his talents to concrete at a South Side youth center. Embedded in this 14-foot grotto are rocks, shells, and other found objects. Warmack enlisted the help of local kids to embellish the structure, and buried beneath it is a time capsule with letters to the children of the future.

Elliott Donnelley Youth Center, 3947 S. Michigan Ave., Chicago, IL 60653

(773) 268-3815

Hours: Monday–Friday 9A.M.–8P.M., Saturday–Sunday 11A.M.–5P.M.

Cost: Free

www.streetlevel.iit.edu/edyc.html

Directions: One block south of Pershing Rd., two blocks east of State St.

Mitch's Place.

The Cross House/Mitch's Place

You can't miss it. Every square inch of this "cottage-style" home is covered in red, black, and silver crosses, most of them emblazoned with famous names.

Back in the late 1970s a man named Mitch Szewczyk started making crosses of wood scraps he found in the street. He wanted to immortalize local politicians and the movie stars of his youth, some of whom were not yet dead. Zsa Zsa Gabor and Jane Byrne might be surprised to find their names on what look like grave markers. Then there are crosses to those who never lived, like Tarzan, Jane, and Zorro. Szewczyk titled his creation "The Cross House," but locals refer to it as "Mitch's Place."

Szewczyk became bedridden in the 1990s and was never able to put up a planned King Kong cross (it was going to be BIG!), nor is he able to maintain the home as well as he'd like. It's still in fairly good shape.

1544 W. Chestnut St., Chicago, IL 60622

Hours: Private residence; always visible

Cost: Free

Directions: Just east of Ashland, six blocks south of Division.

The *Raisin in the Sun* House

A Raisin in the Sun is a classic in American drama, and it is based upon events that happened to the family of its playwright, Lorraine Hansberry. Central to the plot is the story of an African American family that plans a move to a new home in a "restricted" white community.

When Hansberry was just eight years old her father, real estate broker Carl Hansberry, bought a home in west Hyde Park, and the family moved in on May 26, 1937. The neighborhood reacted violently, harassing the children as they played and throwing a brick through the front window. Anna M. Lee, on behalf of the Woodlawn Property Association, filed suit against the Hansberrys, saying they were in violation of a local covenant.

The Circuit Court of Cook County and the Illinois Supreme Court sided with Lee, but the U.S. Supreme Court overturned the lower court's decision in 1941. While *Hansberry v. Lee* did not universally abolish real estate restrictions based upon race, it dealt a major blow to the restrictive practice.

A Raisin in the Sun was published in 1959 to critical acclaim. Whether by coincidence or design, the family's name in the play was Lee, the surname of those who had challenged the Hansberrys in court two decades earlier.

The Hansberrys' former home still stands, though there is no official recognition given this historic piece of property.

Hansberry Home, 6140 S. Rhodes Ave., Chicago, IL 60637

Hours: Always visible

Cost: Free

Directions: Three blocks east of Martin Luther King Dr., two blocks north of 63rd St.

A curse on those who dare scratch your dresser!

Reebie Storage and Moving

The discovery of King Tut's tomb in 1922 led to a surge in public interest surrounding ancient Egyptian culture; Egyptian Revival became the architectural flavor of the month. The Reebie Storage and Moving Company Building, built on North Clark Street in 1923, is an excellent example of this style.

Two pharaohs guard the entrance to the storage facility. Rumors say they resemble John and William Reebie, the two brothers who founded the business and commissioned the building. Hieroglyphics over the entrance translate as "I give protection to your furniture" and "Forever I work for all your regions in daylight and darkness." Now that's service! Where else can you get your sofa protected by an ancient curse?

2325 N. Clark St., Chicago, IL 60614

(773) 878-8100

Hours: Always visible

Cost: Free

Directions: Just south of Fullerton on Clark St.

Playboy Mansion (Midwest)

"If you don't swing, don't ring." This was the motto at the Gold Coast's Playboy Mansion for more than 20 years, and did they ever live up to it. No discussion of funky Chicago homes would be complete without mentioning this place.

Hugh Hefner, former Student Council President of Steinmetz High School, Class of 1944, founded *Playboy* magazine (first called *Stag Party*) on December 10, 1953, with a $600 investment. It was an instant success, and before long Hef had purchased the ultimate groovy bachelor pad, the Playboy Mansion, a mere two blocks from the Archbishop's residence. The mansion had four bedrooms, five fireplaces, an indoor pool, a game room, and a single-lane bowling alley. A firepole dropped visitors into the Underwater Bar, a cozy joint with a window that looked into the swimming pool from below. Bunnies were allowed to stay in the mansion for $50/month, though they had to bunk four to a room and share the bathroom facilities. Hmmm . . . sounds fishy . . .

Hef felt quite comfortable here, lounging around in silk pajamas, smoking his pipe, and guzzling up to 36 bottles of Pepsi a day. He left the building only nine times during one three-year stretch. When questioned why, he confessed, "I don't need to leave. Why should I? I've got more right here now inside this house than most people ever find in a lifetime." A case and a half of Pepsi a day? Maybe he couldn't stray far from a bathroom.

Eventually, the lure of the West Coast became too great and Hefner took up permanent residence in his Los Angeles digs. He donated the mansion to the Art Institute in 1989 and for a while it was used as a dorm, though not with the old Bunny accommodations. Later it was divided into two private residences, which is what it is today.

If you're into *Playboy* history, take a quick stroll over to the former flagship Playboy Club on the Magnificent Mile (919 N. Michigan). The former Palmolive Building was converted to the members-only club in 1960 and it hung on until 1988, when Christie Hefner shut the doors.

Playboy Mansion, 1340 N. State Pkwy., Chicago, IL 60610

Hours: Private residence; always visible

Cost: Free

Directions: Two blocks south of North Ave.

Every day's a holiday at the Christmas House.

The Christmas House

If you ever long for the holiday season in America's six Christmas-free months, stop on by Pilsen's Christmas House. The owner of this home has filled the yard, porch, and roof with artificial trees, stuffed animals, beach balls, and discarded plastic toys for a year-round Yuletide display. Through snow and rain, winter and road construction, the cluttered yard is immaculately maintained and a striking contrast to the bleak railroad yard across the street.

1415 W. 16th St., Chicago, IL 60608

Hours: Private residence; always visible

Cost: Free

Directions: One block west of Blue Island on 16th St.

Hooray for Chicagowood!

Summertime in the Windy City means location shoots for Hollywood studios. It is not uncommon to find blocks worth of neighborhood parking gobbled up by film trailers, but the payoff is seeing Alec Baldwin or Meg Ryan eating in your favorite restaurant on the silver screen. Pinch me.

But Chicago's Hollywood connection is greater than just being a backdrop. It was once the home of the fledgling film industry and has been the training ground of many movie and television stars. And don't forget about the daytime talk shows. When it comes to this form of entertainment, Chicago has cornered the market.

SOME CHICAGO MOVIES

About Last Night	*Looking for Mr. Goodbar*
Backdraft	*The Music Box*
The Breakfast Club	*My Best Friend's Wedding*
Chicago Cab (Hell Cab)	*My Bodyguard*
Class	*Native Son*
The Color of Money	*Natural Born Killers*
Cooley High	*North by Northwest*
Eight Men Out	*Ordinary People*
Endless Love	*Planes, Trains, and Automobiles*
Escape from New York	*Risky Business*
Ferris Bueller's Day Off	*Silver Streak*
Flatliners	*Sixteen Candles*
The Fugitive	*Sleepless in Seattle*
Henry: Portrait of a Serial Killer	*Soul Food*
Hoffa	*The Untouchables*
Hoop Dreams	*Wayne's World*
A League of Their Own	*When Harry Met Sally*

Hollywood before Hollywood.

Essanay Studios

Before there was Hollywood, there was Chicago. During the earliest years of the film industry, the Windy City was home to several studios, the largest of which was Essanay.

Essanay was in business from 1907 to 1917. It was the collaboration of George Spoor and Gilbert "Bronco Billy" Anderson, the S and A of Ess-an-ay. Together they amassed an impressive talent pool of early silent movie stars, including Charlie Chaplin, Gloria Swanson, Ben Turpin, Wallace Beery, Tom Mix, Francis X. Bushman, and, of course, "Bronco Billy." Chaplin worked at Essanay from 1915 to 1916 after leaving Keystone. Here he made 14 movies, including *The Tramp*, at the unheard-of salary of $1,250 a week. But because of creative differences with the owners, Chaplin didn't last long at Essanay.

Uptown was home to the stars and the site of many location shots. The nearby Chicago & North Western tracks along Ravenswood featured heavily in many *Perils of Pauline* cliffhangers. Castlewood Terrace became a one-block forerunner to Beverly Hills. And Gloria Swanson and Wallace Beery were married on the Essanay lot in 1916.

It was the public's insatiable movie appetite and the bitter winters that eventually closed the Chicago studios. Producers needed to film year-round, which was impossible given the climate. So they loaded up their trucks and moved to Beverly. Hills, that is. All that remains of Essanay is the Indian head insignia over the doorway to the old studio building.

1345 W. Argyle, Chicago, IL 60640

Hours: Always visible

Cost: Free

Directions: Between Broadway and Clark on Argyle.

The Music Box

Every movie theater should be this magnificent. One visit to the Music Box and you'll never want to go back to your Octoplex, unless you have a craving for something that doesn't have subtitles or a complicated plot.

The Music Box was built in 1929 and restored in 1983 by Chris Carlo and Bob Chaney. It still has its original Wurlitzer organ, twinkling stars, projected clouds floating across the ceiling, and Mediterranean facades. And if you come early on a Friday or Saturday, a live organist will entertain you before the show, including sing-a-longs!

Gene Siskel once said that his favorite movie seat in Chicago was the first seat in the last row of the Music Box. It's on the left as you enter the right-side entrance.

3733 N. Southport Ave., Chicago, IL 60613

(773) 871-6604

Hours: Call for show times

Cost: $8

www.musicboxtheatre.com

Directions: Between Addison and Irving Park on Southport, west of Clark St.

ARNOLD BENNETT
"Chicago: a mushroom and a filthy suburb of Warsaw."

THEODORE DREISER
"Chicago, a gaudy circus beginning with the two-bit whore in the alley crib."

Blues Brothers Tour

You can argue the point, but *The Blues Brothers* is perhaps Chicago's best "location" movie. Other films have portrayed the city more realistically, but none have done it with such affection. When it comes to Blues Brothers sites, however, the Windy City has not returned the affection; most of the movie locations have been closed, bulldozed, or forgotten.

The movie opens with Elwood picking up Joliet Jake as he's released from **Stateville Correctional Center** (Route 53, Joliet). On the way back to Chicago, Elwood jumps the half-open **East 95th Street Bridge** (95th east of the Skyway, Chicago) in the new Blues Mobile.

The pair end up at the fictitious St. Helen of the Blessed Shroud Orphanage in Calumet City where they learn from The Penguin that the city is about to shut the place down for back taxes. At the urging of Cab Calloway, the janitor, Jake and Elwood head over to the **Pilgrim Baptist Church** (3235 E. 91st St., Chicago) for a service led by James Brown. Jake sees the light and sets out to put "The Band" back together. Heading back to Elwood's flophouse, their car is pulled over by Illinois State Troopers. Elwood ditches the cops using an escape route through the now-abandoned **Dixie Square Mall** (Dixie Highway & 152nd St., Harvey).

They end up back at the **Stag Hotel** downtown (22 W. Van Buren, Chicago) where they are fired upon by Jake's ex-fiancée. The real Stag was *not* blown up by Carrie Fisher's rocket launcher; it was torn down to make way for Pritzker Park across from the Harold Washington Library.

The brothers "rescue" Murph and the Magic Tones from an undisclosed Armada Room at an Interstate Holiday Inn. Next they recruit Mr. Fabulous from his maître d' gig at **Chez Paul** (660 N. Rush, Chicago) after harassing the restaurant's snooty guests. The following day, they run a band of Illinois Nazis into the **Jackson Park Lagoon** (6000 S. Lake Shore Dr., Chicago). The bridge in the movie is actually on a walking path south of the Museum of Science and Industry. The Nazis get the license plate number from the Blues Mobile and join in the movie-long chase, diverted at first by showing up at Elwood's false address: 1060 W. Addison, **Wrigley Field.**

The final band members, Matt "Guitar" Murphy and Blue Lou, work at **Nate's Delicatessen** (807 W. Maxwell) next to the old Maxwell Street Market. Here, Aretha Franklin tells her husband Matt to "Think" about why he shouldn't leave her, but he does anyway. Nate's and the Maxwell

Street Market were run off by the expansion of the University of Illinois at Chicago campus.

With the band back together, the Blue Brothers stop by the **Palace Loan Company** (216 E. 47th St., Chicago) where they pick up musical equipment from Ray Charles, on an IOU, of course. Their first gig is at Bob's Country Bunker in Kokomo, Indiana, substituting for the Good Ol' Boys, unbeknownst to the management. They come across the same Illinois troopers (completely outside their jurisdiction!) who chased the pair through the mall. The troopers ram the Good Ol' Boys' Winnebago and the Blues Brothers escape.

Jake and Elwood hatch a plan to stage a benefit concert. Midway through the show at the fictitious Palace Hotel Ballroom, Jake and Elwood receive a lucrative recording contract and head off to Chicago, followed by police, Nazis, and rednecks.

During the Chicago Loop high-speed chase, the Blues Brothers break through a police barricade at **McCormick Place** (2300 S. Lake Shore Dr.), race along under the **Lake Street** and **Wells Street El** tracks, jump a police car near the **Lyric Opera** (Lower Wacker ramp to Upper Wacker), drive through the lobby windows of the **Richard J. Daley Civic Center**

WHEN STARS ATTACK!

Cabbies and limo drivers beware! Celebrities from both coasts have been known to attack while in the Windy City.

Take **Dan Rather**. He refused to pay a $12.50 fare after his Chicago cabbie got lost in November 1980. The driver then took off down Lake Shore Drive with Dan screaming, "I'm being kidnapped!" to any motorist who would listen. Nobody did.

Butch "Eddie Munster" Patrick beat up his limo driver in November 1990 after the chauffeur also got lost. And if that weren't enough, Patrick reportedly stole the man's wallet (a charge he was later acquitted of). Patrick ended up paying $850 in damages to the driver and a $200 fine. He also received two years' probation with 200 hours of community service.

Finally, **Peter Fonda** stole a limo from a downtown hotel in September 1988 after arguing with the chauffeur, then drove his friends to O'Hare Airport. Chicago police nabbed Fonda there, but the limo service never pressed charges.

and **Plaza** (50 W. Washington), and park outside **City Hall** (121 N. LaSalle). They pay the taxes and the orphanage is saved, but the pair end up back in Joliet.

A replica of the Blues Mobile is sometimes parked outside Dan Aykroyd's **House of Blues** (Marina City, 300 N. State, Chicago).

Good Times

Good Times, a spinoff of *Maude*, which was a spinoff of *All in the Family*, was perhaps Norman Lear's most controversial 1970s sitcom, and that was just among cast members. The show was set in Cabrini Green and was intended to address issues of the African American underclass. It quickly degenerated into a three-syllable interjection: Dy-no-mite! Jimmy "J.J." Walker became an instant star, and the rest of the cast began to grumble. John Amos left the series, turning the TV family's dynamic in an even more stereotypical direction, according to Esther Rolle, who played the matriarch.

The images on the opening credits are close to what you can see today, though some of the abandoned high rises have been demolished in redevelopment plans. Cabrini Green was built on the site of Edwin G. Cooley Vocational High School (1225 N. Sedgwick St.) of *Cooley High* fame. The popular movie, based on the life of Eric Monte (who wrote for *Good Times*), was the inspiration for *What's Happening*.

Cabrini Green is also home to the urban legend of The Candyman. According to the story, a mob executed a man on this site by chopping off his hand, smearing him with honey, and allowing bees to sting him to death. The Candyman kills those who do not believe he exists with his hooked hand. The story was made into two horror movies. It seems a crime that all the *Good Times* difficulty could have been avoided had J.J. mocked the Candyman in an early episode.

Cabrini Green, Division and Halsted, Chicago, IL 60622

Hours: Always visible

Cost: Free

Directions: Northwest of downtown.

SAUL BELLOW
"You can say this about Chicago—there is no hypocrisy problem there. There's no need for hypocrisy. Everyone's proud of being a bastard."

Hi, Bob!

The *Bob Newhart Show*, which ran from 1972 to 1978, was set in Chicago, though there is some debate as to exactly where. One thing's for sure: Bob Hartley's office was located on Michigan Avenue just north of the Wrigley Building. Don't try getting in; the security guard will stop you.

The Hartleys' apartment locale, however, is a bit of a mystery. According to the script, they lived in the "Meridian Beach Apartments," Number 523, in the zip code 60611. The show's exterior shots zoom in on the Buckingham Plaza apartments across the river (in zip code 60601) and focus on the seventh floor, not the fifth. Did the producers think nobody would count?

Buckingham Plaza isn't open to the general public either.

Robert Hartley's Office, 430 N. Michigan Ave., Suite 715, Chicago, IL 60611

The Hartleys' Apartment?, Buckingham Plaza, 360 E. Randolph, Chicago, IL 60601

www.bob-newhart.com

Hill Street Blues

Hill Street Blues was never officially set in any city, but most suspected it was Chicago. Part of the reason was that location shots were often filmed in Chicago and that the precinct shown was an actual Chicago police station. The television series ran from 1981 to 1987. The old police station had a longer run. The Maxwell Street Station was built in the late 1800s as a response to the Haymarket Riot. It had a notorious dungeon for holding and roughing up prisoners, and Al Capone was once briefly detained here. The precinct has recently closed, and the building will soon be used for the campus police at the University of Illinois at Chicago.

Maxwell Street Station, 943 W. Maxwell, Chicago, IL 60608

(312) 996-2830

Hours: Always visible

Cost: Free

Directions: One block south of Roosevelt, three blocks west of Halsted.

STUART ROSENBERG
"Chicago is the ultimate American city—rich, deep, insane."

GEORGE STEEVENS
"Chicago, queen and guttersnipe of cities,
cynosure and cesspool of the world!"

Talk Show Mania

Chicago has long been home to the modern American talk show. According to industry demographics, viewers tend to relate more closely with loudmouth Midwestern folk than they do with loudmouth New York or L.A. residents.

Phil Donahue launched his national show from Chicago in 1977 after relocating from Dayton, Ohio. The early guests were more "mainstream," but Donahue's ratings rose as the topics became more out of the ordinary. This lesson, when followed, has never lost a talk show money.

Oprah Winfrey arrived from Baltimore in January 1984 to host *A.M. Chicago*. When Donahue left for NYC in 1985 (some say he was run out of town by the upstart Winfrey), Oprah's star took off. Though tame today, her early shows were more Geraldo-esque. **Oprah** tickets are difficult to get hold of, but not if you plan in advance. While her tapings are entertaining, the typical 2+ hours you'll spend in security and the preshow holding tank will wear you down before the lights come up.

Tickets to **Jenny Jones** and **Jerry Springer** aren't as hard to come by, as long as you don't count the cost to your pride. These shows are produced in adjoining studios at the NBC Tower. If you can't decide which of the two you want to see, ask yourself which would be less painful: listening to Springer's lousy jokes and Elvis impersonations during commercial breaks, or having to sit through yet another "teenage makeover" with Jones.

The Oprah Winfrey Show, 1058 W. Washington Blvd., Chicago, IL 60607

Harpo Productions/Oprah Tickets, PO Box 909715, Chicago, IL 60690

(312) 591-9222

www.oprah.com

The Jenny Jones Show, 454 N. Columbus Dr., Chicago, IL 60611

(312) 836-9485

www.jennyjones.warnerbros.com

The Jerry Springer Show, 454 N. Columbus Dr., Chicago, IL 60611

(312) 321-5365

www.universalstudios.com/tv/jerryspringer

LOUELLA PARSONS
"There are two types of people in this country.
There are the ones who love Chicago and the ones who
think it is unmitigated hell."

Don't blame the cow.

Disaster-rama
Mrs. O'Leary's Fire, The Great Flood,
and Other Catastrophes

Chicago loves disasters. Why else would the city commemorate the Great
Chicago Fire and the Fort Dearborn Massacre on its flag? That's right,
two of the flag's four stars signify those tragedies; the other two stars are
for the city's two World Fairs.

So if Chicago doesn't have any difficulty bringing up these horrific events, why should you, the humble traveler, worry if visiting them is in poor taste? Lighten up. Enjoy the carnage.

The Great Chicago Fire

The most popular explanation for the Chicago Fire's origin has been all but debunked, but here it is: Mrs. Catherine O'Leary's cow kicked over a lantern while she was milking it on October 8, 1871. It was 9:30P.M. During the next 27 hours, a conflagration leveled 3.5 square miles of the Midwest's largest city, killing 250, destroying 17,450 buildings, and leaving more than 94,000 homeless, one-third of the city's population. Ironically, the O'Learys weren't left homeless; their home survived the fire. The flames kicked up a 60-mph draft inward as it gobbled 65 acres an hour. Heat from the flames could be felt 100 miles away, and the fire's glow was spotted from Lake Geneva, Wisconsin, and across Lake Michigan.

Citizens fled the wall of flames, running out into Lake Michigan or into Lincoln Park, where they huddled in recently exhumed graves at the old City Cemetery. Buildings were blown up along Congress Street by General Sheridan to stop the fire, but it didn't halt its advance. A small faction of the male population used the opportunity to raid abandoned saloons, putting themselves in no position to fight or outrun the approaching flames. The fire didn't burn itself out until it reached Fullerton Avenue on the North Side.

So how did the fire really start? Several theories have been presented. Everyone agrees today that O'Leary was not in the barn when it ignited. At the time, some pointed the finger not at the cow but on a group of Irish youths who had gone to O'Leary's barn to get some milk to make their alcoholic "punch" and started the fire by mistake. Today, some accuse O'Leary's neighbor, Daniel "Peg Leg" Sullivan, who was all too eager to accuse poor old Kate. Sullivan apparently was lying when he told an Inquiry Board that he saw the fire start in O'Leary's barn, a barn that was actually blocked from his view by a two-story home.

The most interesting theory presented blames a heavenly body: a comet! Author Mel Waskin, in the book *Mrs. O'Leary's Comet!*, claims Biela's Comet broke into two pieces in 1845, one of which crashed to earth when it circled back around in 1871. Interestingly enough, more than 24 towns around the Midwest were leveled by three major fires that all started at about the same moment, including Peshtigo, Wisconsin, and Manistee, Michigan. Many witnesses claim to have heard a thunderous roar *before* the fires began and to have seen a mysterious rain of sand *during* the fire. It sounds wacky, but the book is quite convincing.

A bronze, flame-shaped monument to the victims, called *Pillar of Fire*, now stands at the former site of O'Leary's barn. It is also the location of the fire department's training center.

Pillar of Fire Monument, 558 W. DeKoven St. (137 before street renumbering), Chicago, IL 60607

Hours: Always visible

Cost: Free

Directions: One block north of Roosevelt Rd., two blocks east of the Dan Ryan Expressway.

Other Chicago Fires

While the Great Chicago Fire was disastrous, it was not the most deadly fire in Chicago history. Both a fire at the Iroquois Theater and a 1995 heat wave racked up more casualties. So if you're a fire buff, check out these other Chicago sites, or consider taking a Chicago Historical Fire Tour hosted by Ken Little, retired CFD Senior Dispatcher (Contact: Chris Greve, 1490 Willow St., Lake Forest, IL 60045). They run several tours each year.

- The **Iroquois Theater**'s (24 W. Randolph) backdrop caught fire during a performance of *Mr. Bluebeard* on December 30, 1903. Over 600 theatergoers were burned or trampled, most of them women and children. The Iroquois had been dubbed "absolutely fireproof" during its grand opening only 27 days earlier. The asbestos safety curtain jammed as it was being dropped. The fire led to the first red exit signs, fireproofed scenery, and the practice of having exit doors opening outward with "panic bars." The newly rehabilitated Oriental Theater is located on the site today. A monument to the victims is located in the Montrose Cemetery (5400 N. Pulaski).
- Goodyear's first dirigible, the *Wing Foot*, crashed through the skylight of the **Illinois Trust and Savings Bank** (231 S. LaSalle, site of the Bank of America Building today) on July 21, 1919, after an engine set the hydrogen-filled balloon on fire. It was its maiden voyage. Twelve died, nine of them in the bank, and many more were injured.

- The **Haber Corporation** plant in Chicago (908 W. North Ave.) burned after an explosion on April 16, 1953. It was in the process of being remodeled and the front entrances were blocked. Thirty-five workers perished.
- The **LaSalle Hotel** (LaSalle & Madison) burned on June 6, 1946. Sixty-one people died after burning, asphyxiating, or jumping to their deaths. Owners had billed the hotel as "the largest, safest, and most modern hotel west of New York." The structure was repaired and used as a hotel until it was razed in 1976.
- Three nuns and ninety-two children perished on December 1, 1958, when **Our Lady of the Angels** parochial school (909 N. Avers) caught fire. All public and private schools were ordered to install sprinklers after the tragedy; none could be "grandfathered" to avoid compliance as Our Lady of the Angels had been. Twenty-five of the victims were buried near a memorial at Queen of Heaven Catholic Cemetery in Hillside (Roosevelt & Wolf Rd.). A new school has been built near the site (3820 W. Iowa).
- The **Paxton Hotel** (1432 N. LaSalle) caught fire on March 16, 1993, killing 19 residents. The SRO hotel was not required to install sprinklers, in order to keep the rents reasonable for its more low-income residents.
- Over 700 Chicago residents died during a July 1995 heat wave. Though not a fire, it sure felt like Hell.

DEBUNKING A MYTH

One of the buildings to survive the Chicago fire, **Holy Family Catholic Church** (1080 W. Roosevelt Rd.), still commemorates its survival. Seven candles (today, lightbulbs) are kept lit in front of a statue of the Virgin Mary, Our Lady of Perpetual Help. The candles fulfill a solemn oath made by the church's pastor, Father Arnold Damen. He prayed to the Virgin Mary as the flames headed for Holy Family. Damen was in New York City at the time but had gotten the news by telegraph. Parishioners claimed the flames miraculously turned, but any student of the fire knows the story to be false. From the beginning the flames burned toward Lake Michigan, not inland toward Holy Family. The church was never in any danger! Still, the lightbulbs remain illuminated, just in case.

The Great Chicago Flood

It happened on April 13, 1992. Around midday, basements of many Chicago skyscrapers started filling with water. Lots of water. City crews soon noticed a whirlpool near the Kinzie Street Bridge—somebody had pulled the cork on the Chicago River!

More accurately, somebody had punctured a hole in the river, and that somebody was the Great Lakes Dredge and Dock Company. They held the contract to put pilings on the waterway and had pounded several posts through the riverbed and into a network of antiquated freight tunnels running beneath the Loop. It took crews several days and many attempts to plug the hole, but not before 134 million gallons flooded 50 downtown office buildings. By the time the cleanup was over, officials estimated the city had suffered $1 billion in damages and lost revenue.

Kinzie Street Bridge, 450 W. Kinzie, Chicago, IL 60610

Hours: Always visible

Cost: Free

Directions: South of the bridge, due west of the Merchandise Mart.

Eastland Death Site

The United States' second most deadly inland marine tragedy occurred downtown only a few feet from the banks of the Chicago River. The *Eastland* was docked at the Clark Street Bridge along Wacker Drive between LaSalle and Clark on July 24, 1915. About 2,500 employees of the Western Electric Company squeezed onto the boat meant for half that number. The top-heavy ship tipped toward the dock, the passengers shifted to the other side at the same moment the crew flooded ballast tanks, and the craft capsized in the opposite direction. In all, 812 people died, including 22 entire families.

Interestingly enough, public reaction to the *Titanic* disaster might have contributed to the tragedy. The *Eastland* was overloaded with lifeboats on its upper deck, retrofitted after the *Titanic*, which made the craft unstable.

Some of the tragedy's victims were sent to the 2nd Regiment Armory (1054 W. Washington) where a makeshift morgue had been opened. This same building houses Oprah's Harpo Studios today, and the talk show host has claimed she has felt the spirits' presence. One of those who didn't die in the wreck was George Halas (who would later become the Bears football coach). He arrived at the dock too late because of a baseball game in Indiana. Lucky George.

Eastland memorial plaque, 180 W. Wacker Street, Chicago, IL 60601

Hours: Always visible

Cost: Free

Directions: Along the Wacker walkway between the LaSalle and Clark St. bridges.

Three Submarines and Something Else

You wouldn't expect to hear a strange submarine story associated with Chicago, but there are actually three, maybe four.

Salvage crews were dredging the river following the *Eastland* tragedy and they snagged a small craft on the riverbed. It turned out to be a one-man submarine with two skeletons inside, one human and one dog. Investigators believed it to be the wreck of an experimental vessel made by Lodner Phillips from Indiana. He had sold the imperfect contraption to William Nissen, most likely the victim found inside. The craft was dubbed the *Foolkiller* and put on display, along with the two skeletons.

The *Eastland*, on the other hand, was righted and eventually rechristened the USS *Wilmette*. It served as a navy gunboat in WWI and a trainer out of Navy Pier following the war. At the same time, a confiscated German UC-97 sub needed to be scuttled under terms of the Treaty of Versailles, and it was the USS *Wilmette* that sent it to the bottom of Lake Michigan, 20 miles off the Chicago shore.

Another sub, a Nazi U-505, was captured off the West African coast near the end of WWII. The sub was donated to the Museum of Science and Industry where it's on display today, along with several fake crates of sauerkraut.

ANOTHER CHICAGO WATER DISASTER

Two hundred and ninety-seven Wisconsin Democrats died on September 8, 1860, when the *Lady Elgin* steamer collided with a schooner, the *Augusta of Oswego*, and sank in Lake Michigan. Only 98 people made the 10-mile swim to shore. The tragedy spurred the construction of the **Grosse Point Lighthouse** in Evanston. The wreckage was discovered in 1989 and plans are underway to either salvage the ship or make it an underwater museum.

The final submarine, if it is that, sits just inside the Chicago River locks in the ship-turning basin. The 31-foot-long object is shaped like a hotdog and has a square hatch in its side. It is made of wood, banded with iron straps, and has a pipe running from end to end. Nobody knows what it is or how it got there. The Coast Guard will drag the . . . whatever . . . out into the middle of the lake in the near future.

Museum of Science and Industry, 5700 S. Lake Shore Dr., Chicago, IL 60637-2093

(773) 684-1414

Hours: Monday–Friday 9:30A.M.–4P.M. (5:30P.M. summers), Saturday–Sunday 9:30A.M.–5:30P.M.

Cost: Adults $7, Seniors(65+) $6, Kids(3–11) $3.50, Thursdays free

www.msichicago.org

Directions: In Jackson Park off Lake Shore Drive at 57th St.

Will somebody please let me out?
Photo by author, courtesy of the Museum of Science and Industry, Chicago.

Chicago Public Transportation Disasters

Chicago has been called the Crossroads of the Nation, and where roads cross, there are bound to be collisions. If you're interested in death and mayhem, here are a few sites of Chicago's most deadly mishaps:

- A CTA streetcar struck a gasoline truck at 63rd and State on May 25, 1950, incinerating 33 commuters.
- A metal CTA El train rear-ended a wooden El at the Granville station (Granville & Broadway) on November 24, 1936, killing 11 and reducing one car to kindling.
- Two Illinois Central trains collided near the 27th Street Station (27th St. & Lake Shore Drive) on October 30, 1972, killing 45 passengers and crew and injuring 350 more.
- A four-car CTA El train fell off the Loop tracks (Lake & Wabash) after colliding with another train on February 4, 1977. The accident killed 11.

Chicago Air Disasters

What goes up, must come down. In Chicago, some have come down a little harder than others. There are two airports in Chicago: one is the busiest in the world, and the other is jammed between South Side row houses. Sounds like two recipes for TRAVEL DISASTER!

Oh-My-God O'Hare

- When an American Airlines DC-10's left-wing engine fell off after takeoff from O'Hare on May 25, 1979, all 271 passengers and crew were killed along with two on the ground. It was the worst single-plane accident in U.S. history. One person who wasn't killed was Lindsay "The Bionic Woman" Wagner. Wagner and her mother were scheduled to fly on American's doomed Flight 191 but had an eerie feeling and changed their reservations. Had Wagner been on the flight, and had she been bionic, she might have been able to climb out on the wing and hold the engine in place long enough to make an emergency landing. Some people claim they can hear the cries of the dead and crumpling metal at the spot where the plane hit the ground, a field a half-mile from the end of the runway.
- A Delta Convair and a North Central DC-9 collided on the runway at O'Hare on December 20, 1972. Nine people on the DC-9 died.

- When a North Central Convair 580 crashed into a hanger at O'Hare on December 27, 1968, 27 passengers and crew perished. The pilot had become confused by the fog.
- A Northwest Orient Lockheed Electra crashed after takeoff from O'Hare on September 17, 1961, killing 37. The plane hit the ground in Bensenville.

Murderous Midway

- When a United Airlines 737 crashed into a street of row houses (Lawndale & 17th St.) near Midway on December 8, 1972, Dorothy Hunt, the wife of Watergate co-conspirator E. Howard Hunt, was among the 45 killed. Her purse was found with $10,000 worth of sequential $100 bills, a likely payoff.
- Seventy-eight people died on September 1, 1961, when a TWA Lockheed 1049 crashed in Hinsdale after taking off from Midway. A bolt in the plane's elevator booster had fallen out.
- A commuter helicopter crashed into the western half of Forest Home Cemetery in Forest Park on July 27, 1960, after its main rotor detached. Thirteen commuters traveling from Midway to O'Hare were killed.
- A Braniff pilot clipped a service station sign near Midway with the wing of his Convair on July 7, 1955, causing the plane to crash into the foggy airfield. Twenty-two died.
- A military B-24 bomber crashed near 73rd and Central Park on May 20, 1943, killing 22 crewmen. By an unfortunate coincidence, a gasoline storage tank stood on the same site. The plane was attempting to land at Midway.
- Seven passengers and three crew members were killed when a United Airlines DC-3 crashed near Midway on December 4, 1940, heavily laden with ice. Investigators also believe the plane might have stalled.

RUDYARD KIPLING
"Having seen (Chicago), I urgently desire never to see it again. It is inhabited by savages. Its water is the water of the Hughli, and its air is dirt."

Riot On, Chicago!
Any Excuse to Get Rowdy

Chicago has the unique distinction of hosting two of history's most famous riots. The first, the Haymarket Riot, led to the eight-hour work-day and May Day labor holidays. The second, the 1968 Democratic Convention melee, was the first riot broadcast live on national TV. In many respects, Haymarket and 1968 are standards by which other riots are measured . . . and there have been plenty of others.

The City has never been proud of this history and has made some efforts to prevent future disorders. Nine Aldermen used the city's "incitement to riot" statute to remove, by force, the painting "Mirth and Girth" from the Art Institute. It depicted Harold Washington in women's underwear and was based on an unsubstantiated rumor, now Urban Legend, that the mayor was found to be wearing women's underwear after suffering his fatal heart attack. Of all the riots that could have been averted, the Aldermen had to choose this one! It might have been the most interesting to watch.

Haymarket Riot

On May 4, 1886, a group of workers and anarchists gathered in Haymarket Square to protest working conditions at the McCormick Farm Machinery Works (Blue Island & Western) where two protesters had been shot the day before. Central to their grievances was the call for an eight-hourwork-day. By all accounts, the gathering was peaceful; even Chicago Mayor Carter Harrison stopped by for a look. Then the police arrived.

A 176-man police battalion approached the workers near the corner of Randolph and Des Plaines. Without warning, a bomb was thrown at the police. One policeman was killed immediately. All hell broke loose, and before it was over, six other cops and four civilians (probably more) were either dead or mortally wounded. An investigation later suggested that most of the police casualties were shot in the back by other trigger-happy cops during the fracas.

Each side blamed the other for the explosion, though it was never determined who was responsible. That didn't mean, however, that nobody was indicted for the crime. Eight men, all anarchists and/or labor organizers, were tried and convicted. Four were eventually hanged on Black Friday, November 11, 1887: August Spies, Albert Parsons, Adolph

Fischer, and George Engel. A fifth, Louis Lingg, was scheduled for the gallows but committed suicide in his cell the day before. Lingg bit down on a dynamite cap smuggled into his cell—Ouch! Before the trap door opened, August Spies shouted, "The day will come when our silence will be more powerful than the voices you are throttling today." George Engel was less prophetic but more upbeat, shouting, "Hurrah for anarchy! This is the happiest moment of my life!" Yikes. Some life.

Three men who received prison sentences—Michael Schwab, Samuel Fielden, and Oscar Neebe—were pardoned in 1893 by Illinois Governor John Peter Altgeld. Though scorned and soundly defeated in the next election, Altgeld proclaimed, "No man's ambition has the right to stand in the way of performing a simple act of justice."

For many years, a monument stood at the site of the riot. It was dedicated not to the workers looking for a fair deal, but to the police who shot one another in the backs. The statue of a policeman, arm outstretched, topped a pedestal that read, "In the name of the people of Illinois, I command peace!," the words supposedly uttered by Police Captain Ward before the riot started.

The monument had its critics and had to be shuffled around Chicago for years. At each new location it was threatened by vandals, workers, or Yippies. It was bombed in 1890, rammed by a proletarian streetcar driver in 1927, and blown up by the Weathermen in 1969 and by another unnamed bomber in 1970. It was then moved to the lobby of the Chicago Police Academy, where it stands today. You can see a copy at the American Police Center and Museum (1717 S. State St.). What remained of its base was jackhammered away before the 1996 Democratic National Convention. You can still see the shadow of the pedestal in the sidewalk.

Former site of the Haymarket monument, 600 W. Randolph St., Chicago, IL 60661

Hours: Always visible

Cost: Free

dwardmac.pitzer.edu/anarchist_archives/haymarket/Haymarket.html

Directions: At Randolph and Des Plaines in the west Loop.

D. H. LAWRENCE
"It rained and fogged in Chicago and muddy-flowing people oozed thick in the canyon-beds of the streets. Yet it seemed to me more alive and more real than New York."

RAGE AGAINST THE (CHICAGO) MACHINE

If you think Hubert Humphrey getting nominated is enough to send this city into turmoil, consider some of Chicago's other rage-fests:

Lager Beer Hall Riots—April 21, 1855

When annual beer hall license fees jumped from $50 to $300, local drunks got behind the beer hall owners ("high-brow" whiskey parlors were exempt) and threatened to burn down City Hall . . . with Know-Nothing Mayor Dr. Levi Boone inside! After marching on the mayor, a riot near the Clark Street Bridge downtown ended with one dead and many injured.

Pullman Riots—July 1894

After a string of pay cuts and massive firings (with no reduction in their company-town rents), workers at the Pullman Palace Car Company went on strike on May 11, 1894. George Pullman responded, "There is nothing to negotiate." Sympathetic railroad workers refused to work on trains with Pullman Sleeping Cars. The *Chicago Tribune* fanned the flames with exaggerated tales of union violence. Federal troops (sent in by Attorney General Richard Olney, a former railroad lawyer) were called in to protect the plant and fired into a crowd. Three children died. Riots erupted all over the South Side; 13 striking workers were killed. Businesses were looted, mostly by the soldiers and opportunistic jerks not involved in the dispute.

27th Street Beach Race Riots—July 27–31, 1919

African American teenager Eugene Williams tried to swim ashore after drifting into a "whites only" area, the 27th Street Beach, from 25th. A mob forced him back out into the water where he drowned after being hit in the head with a rock. Bathers from white and black beaches began battling in what turned out to be a five-day race riot. Cars of white Chicagoans would drive through black areas and shoot residents at random. Before it ended, 23 blacks and 15 whites were dead. More than 500 Chicagoans were injured and 2,000 left homeless.

Rent Strike Riot—August 3, 1931

After a black family's eviction from their home at 5016 S. Dearborn St., residents launched a neighborhood rent strike. During a demonstration, tensions flared and a fight broke out between white bystanders and black marchers. Three marchers were killed and three police were injured.

Memorial Day Massacre—May 30, 1937
Police tried to break up a picket line outside the Republic Steel Corporation plant on the South Side, and when that didn't work, they fired into the crowd. Ten strikers were killed, most of them shot in the back. An investigation criticized "excessive force" on the part of police.

MLK Assassination Riot—April 7–10, 1968
Like many northern cities, Chicago erupted following the assassination of Martin Luther King, Jr. in 1968. During the three-day riot, 11 were killed, mostly on the West Side. Mayor Richard Daley issued his infamous "shoot-to-kill" (arsonists) and "shoot to maim" (looters) order.

Days of Rage—October 8–11, 1969
In what has since been described as a citywide temper tantrum, the Weathermen ran through Chicago's Gold Coast breaking windows, beating bystanders, and causing havoc. They were protesting the trial of the Chicago 8, racism, and the rich. Before it was over, three Weathermen were shot, 57 police and countless citizens injured, and $1 million of property damage inflicted.

Sly and the Family Stone Non-concert—July 27, 1970
When Sly and the Family Stone failed to show up for a Grant Park concert, 50,000 fans took it out on the city, injuring 128 police and 33 of their own.

Disco Demolition Derby—July 12, 1979
Disc jockey Steve Dahl, who had been justifiably replaced by a disco format, staged a PR stunt at Comiskey Park (3500 S. Wentworth) during the break at a White Sox/Detroit Tigers doubleheader. Disco haters were told to bring dance records to the game where they would be blown up. The explosion left a crater in center field. Many fans were injured by flying LPs after Bee Gee–hating rockers began flinging records around the stadium. The second game was canceled.

The Police Riots

The 1968 Democratic National Convention was a riot waiting to happen: a springtime of political assassinations, an escalating war in Vietnam, long-haired hippie types "invading" the city, rumors that Chicago's water supply would be dosed with LSD, an intransigent mayor with a chip on his shoulder, and a whole lot of cops who weren't used to taking no for an answer. And there wasn't just one riot, there were dozens. Here are a few of the larger melees, if you'd like to relive them.

Sunday, August 25: At midnight, police "clear" crowds from the south end of Lincoln Park. Protesters move down Clark Street through Old Town and battle with police at the Michigan Avenue Bridge.

Monday, August 26: Protesters climb onto the General John Logan statue in Grant Park, just southeast of the Conrad Hilton, until peeled off by police. That night, police use tear gas to clear Lincoln Park.

Tuesday, August 27: The Illinois National Guard "controls" Grant Park this night while the Chicago police bash heads in Lincoln Park. Allen Ginsberg tries to stop the riot by suggesting everyone chant a mantra. It doesn't work.

Wednesday, August 28: Ten thousand protesters converge on the Grant Park bandshell. The City denies them a permit to march. A flag south of the bandshell is lowered by demonstrators and the cops move in to mace and club everyone in sight. Protesters regroup and escort a Mule Train from the Poor People's Campaign through the fracas by the Hilton. Demonstrators throw feces at the police. A 20-minute riot, the "Battle for Balbo," takes place at the corner of Michigan and Balbo. It would later be called a "police riot" by the Walker Commission.

Thursday, August 29: Crowds try to march to the Amphitheater where the Convention is being held but are turned back at 16th and State by National Guard troops; they return to Grant Park. Dick Gregory invites them to come down to his place, and the second march is turned back at 18th and Michigan.

Chicago Hilton and Towers (formerly the Conrad Hilton), 720 S. Michigan Ave., Chicago, IL 60605

(800) HILTONS

Hours: Always open

Cost: Free

Directions: At Michigan Ave. and Balbo.

God and the Devil Come to Town
Holy and Unholy Visitations

If given the choice to equate Chicago with Heaven or Hell, most people choose Hell. It is, after all, the birthplace of both Anton LaVey and the Devil Baby of Hull House. Ashley Montague once said, "Hell has been described as a pocket edition of Chicago," and Carl Sandburg concurred: "Here is the difference between Dante, Milton, and me. They wrote about Hell and never saw the place. I wrote about Chicago after looking over the place for years and years."

Still, Chicago has had its fair share of visitors from on high. In the 1980s a naked man claiming he was Jesus Christ jumped into a moving convertible on Chicago's Lake Shore Drive. Another self-appointed Messiah set fire to two cars during rush hour on the Michigan Avenue Bridge, screaming, "I come in the name of Jesus Christ, my father, to save America!"

Whichever camp you tend to believe, Chicago has plenty of holy and unholy places to visit.

Mother Cabrini Death Site

"From this chair the soul of St. Frances Xavier Cabrini took flight to heaven." So reads the plaque on the back of a simple wicker chair in Columbus Hospital. This is not some sort of rocket chair, but the chair in which the patron saint of immigrants died on December 22, 1917.

Mother Cabrini of the Missionary Sisters of the Sacred Heart founded the hospital in 1905, and it was here that she spent her final days packing toys for the poor children at Assumption School. What a saint! Literally. She was canonized on July 7, 1946. One of her miracles? A young woman's varicose veins were cured when she put on Mother Cabrini's cotton stockings instead of the support hose the doctor had prescribed.

In addition to the wicker chair, they've got the habit she wore the day before she died, her eyeglasses, and a floor mat that caught a drop of her blood when her soul departed this earth.

Columbus Hospital, 2520 N. Lakeview St., Chicago, IL 60614

(773) 388-7338

Hours: Daily 10A.M.–Noon, 1–3:30P.M.

Cost: Free

Directions: Two blocks north of Fullerton, next to the chapel inside the south entrance to the hospital.

God on the Radio

For the money, there is no better theatrical entertainment in Chicago than the radio drama *UNSHACKLED!*, recorded at the Pacific Garden Mission each Saturday. They have been producing the program without interruption since 1950, so they know what they're doing.

UNSHACKLED!, is a throwback to the early days of radio. Each episode is a new "true story" of a sinner or sufferer who finds redemption, and while that might not sound like a barrel of laughs, its surprisingly entertaining. At least two-thirds of each play chronicles the downward spiral of random tragedy and/or sin of the main character, every event punctuated with a soap-opera burst of organ music. Just when you think somebody can't endure another hardship, they're stricken with a new disease, mugged on a street corner, or they watch their home burn to the ground.

And then the main character finds God. This doesn't always free them from their troubles, but at least they feel better about their life-threatening disease or dire situation. And, of course, they are unshackled from the SIN that got them in the mess in the first place.

The radio plays are produced 17 weeks in advance of their air dates, allowing Pacific Garden Mission to economically distribute it throughout their station network. They point out that the actors in the plays are union professionals and not all of them are "saved." That's probably just as well; if everyone was "saved" there would be no material for next week's episode of . . . *UNSHACKLED!*

Pacific Garden Mission, 646 S. State St., Chicago, IL 60605

(312) 922-1462

Hours: Saturdays at 4:30P.M.; seating begins at 4:15

Cost: Free

www.pgm.org

Directions: Two blocks south of Congress on State.

STUDS TERKEL
"Chicago is not the most corrupt American city—
it's the most theatrically corrupt."

Weeping and Oozing Around Town

Weeping statues and icons are nothing new in Chicago. The apparitions have never been as exotic as Jesus on a tortilla or Mother Theresa in a cinnamon roll, but what they lack in quality they more than make up in frequency. Here are just a few.

A painting of the Virgin Mary in St. Nicholas Albanian Orthodox Church began weeping from her eyes and between her fingers on December 6, 1986, "crying for Albania," as the official story went. Not only did the painting cry, but the image of the Virgin seemed to be red-eyed and puffy as well. This went on for seven months, during which time her fingers dripped water and a cross appeared on her forehead. Due to ample parking at the adjacent Brickyard Mall, attendance was heavy. The icon stopped weeping in July 1987, then did a brief return engagement in July 1988. At that time, the tears she produced were used to anoint 19 other icons in Pennsylvania and they all began weeping, too.

St. Nicholas Albanian Orthodox Church, 2701 N. Narragansett Ave., Chicago, IL 60639

(773) 889-4282

Hours: Venerations Wednesday, Saturday, and Sunday 10A.M.–4P.M.

Cost: Free

Directions: One block south of Diversey on the east side of the Brickyard Mall.

Details are sketchy, but some parishioners at St. Adrian's Church on the South Side still remember when the 1,700-year-old remains of St. Maximina, a first-class relic, began oozing watery blood back in May 1970. Apparently it's easier to get blood from a saint than a turnip.

St. Adrian's Church, 7000 S. Fairfield, Chicago, IL 60629

(773) 434-3223

Hours: Masses Sunday at 8, 10, and 11:30A.M.

Cost: Free

Directions: One block east of California, one block north of 71st St.

Several icons at Apanacio and St. John on the North Side began weeping in the early 1990s. The thought of decorating with a channel to heaven was too much for one sticky-fingered individual—somebody stole the icons. They were later returned, their tears no longer flowing. The church has since been disbanded.

Apanacio and St. John, 1416 W. Waveland, Chicago, IL 60613

Hours: Torn down

Cost: Free

Suburban churches have also gotten into the weeping act. A fiberglass crucifix in Hillside's Queen of Heaven Cemetery bleeds on occasion and turns colors, according to pilgrims. You can find it in the southeast "Military Section" of the cemetery; it's usually surrounded by the kneeling faithful. Some visitors claim to have seen the Virgin hovering by the cross, some have seen the sun "spin," and others have had their silver rosaries turned to gold. If you visit this site, be sure to talk to some of the gathered. Many have albums of miracle photos showing angels in the clouds, light beams shooting out from Jesus' wounds, blood dripping from the statue, and the occasional fingers over their lenses.

The apparitions began after local resident Joseph Reinholtz returned from Medjugorje in 1987. The Virgin appeared to him and restored his eyesight. She then showed up every day as he prayed at the Queen of Heaven crucifix. Word got around and soon hundreds visited the cross each day . . . except Tuesday. Mary did not appear on Tuesday at the request of the Archdiocese; they wanted Reinholtz to give them a day of rest and the Virgin complied. They also issued a statement on July 26, 1991, that stated their policy on the apparitions: "The Church does not readily accept as authentic any claims made by an individual." Mary seemed peeved, because she has almost never returned, especially now that Reinholtz is dead.

Be sure to visit the Hillside Apparitions Web site and read Reinholtz's accounts of his interactions with the mother of Jesus. On one occasion, Mary and two angels rode with him to Detroit in his car. Mary sat in the front seat between Reinholtz and a female companion. The angels sat in back. Mary claimed she had never ridden in an auto before, and given her behavior on the return trip, it's a good thing. Coming back from Detroit she vanished, then reappeared flying through the air above the car and landed on the hood!

Queen of Heaven Cemetery, 1400 S. Roosevelt Rd., Hillside, IL 60162

(708) 449-8300

Hours: Rosaries Monday, Wednesday–Saturday 9A.M., Sunday 10A.M.

Cost: Free

web.frontier.net/Apparitions/hillside.html

Directions: West of Wolf Rd. and south of Roosevelt Rd.

OSCAR WILDE "Your city looks positively dreary."

Mary pays a visit to Hanover Park.

An iconic panel of the Virgin Mary began weeping oil at the beginning of Holy Week in suburban Cicero on April 22, 1994. Eight Orthodox bishops examined the tears and declared, unanimously, that it was a miracle! Just to be sure they weren't being fooled by the Devil, they performed an exorcism on the icon. Mary continued to cry, so she had to be the real thing. The icon has since been renamed Our Lady of Cicero. The tears were not enough to prevent a recent fire.

St. George's Antiochan Orthodox Church, 1220 S. 60th Court, Cicero, IL 60804

(708) 656-2927

Hours: Services Saturday 5:30P.M., Sunday 9:30, and 10:30A.M.

Cost: Free

Directions: One block south of Roosevelt, one block west of Austin.

Finally, in a less-holy setting, the Virgin of Guadalupe made a visit to a Hanover Park apartment complex in 1997. Her image appeared out of the shadows as a security light shined on the side of a building. When the light was turned off, Mary took off, too. But the people remained. Today, in the far southwest end of the parking lot, a tent leans against the building where it all happened. Inside are hundreds of votive candles surrounding a statue of the Virgin of Guadalupe.

2420 Glendale Terrace, Hanover Park, IL 60103

Hours: Always visible

Cost: Free

Directions: One block north of Lake St. (Rte. 20) off Walnut.

The Wall of Turin

Could it be? Perhaps? Yes? A simple brick wall in Wicker Park seems to have the faint image of Jesus oozing from its bricks! A miracle? The Wall of Turin?

No, just the work of Robert Heinecken, a local artist. Heinecken painted the side of his building to elicit responses from unsuspecting passersby. Even up close, the bricks don't look altered, just naturally discolored. That alone is a miracle.

Now that you know the secret, you've got the perfect prop to play a trick of your own. Bring your friends out to dinner and park near the wall. After you eat and everyone's loosened up, pass by the image and do a double take. Ask your friends what they see. Have a vision. Fall to your knees. Convert on the spot.

1801 W. Wabansia, Chicago, IL 60622

Hours: Always visible

Cost: Free

Directions: At the corner of Wabansia and Wood Sts.

Devil in a Little Parish

It isn't just Mary and Jesus that come to visit Chicago's churches; the Devil has dropped by, too. In fact, he's come to St. Michael's on the North Side twice.

According to parishioners' stories, the first time Satan dropped by he came in the form of an old woman. She reportedly followed a priest out of the church, but he figured out who she was when he noticed her cloven hooves. The padre chased the Evil One off.

So much for learning from experience. When the Devil returned in the 1980s in a hooded cloak and tried to take communion during mass, he again forgot to cover his goatlike tootsies: No shoes. No toes. No service!

St. Michael's Church, 1633 N. Cleveland Ave., Chicago, IL 60614

(312) 642-2498

Hours: Services Saturday 6P.M., Sunday 8A.M., 9:15A.M., 11A.M., and 7P.M.

Cost: Free

Directions: One block north of North Ave., five blocks west of LaSalle.

The Archangel Michael

So is the Devil alive and causing trouble in the Windy City? Not if you believe the statue in the entryway of St. Mary of the Angels Church. The sculpture depicts the Archangel Michael standing on the Devil with a spear jammed into the Dark One's throat. Just the thing you want to see on a Sunday morning.

St. Mary of the Angels Church, 1850 N. Hermitage Ave., Chicago, IL 60622

(773) 278-2644

Hours: Daily 7A.M.–7:15P.M.

Cost: Free

Directions: Two blocks south of Armitage, three blocks west of Ashland.

Pushin' Up the Wild Onions
Dead in Chicago

Being dead in Chicago isn't all bad. For one thing, you can still vote. For another, the worms that eat you may be the same worms that devoured some famous Americans, as long as you choose the right spot to be buried.

One of Chicago's most visible gravesites isn't a gravesite at all—it's home plate at Wrigley Field! Songwriter Steve "City of New Orleans" Goodman asked that his ashes be interred beneath home plate in a song titled "A Dying Cub Fan's Last Request," and since he was the first and only celebrity who had asked for the privilege, the stadium allowed it.

Chicago's least visible grave is that of Morris the Cat. It may be just an urban myth, but word is Morris I is buried in the backyard of his Chicago-based trainer.

If Morris and Goodman are displeased with spending eternity in Chicago, they're not saying much. It is at least some measure of their civic pride that they vote in local, state, and national elections when the Ward bosses need them.

Chris Farley Death Site

When you die a premature, tragic death, folks come out of the woodwork to praise you and contemplate what might have been had you survived. After 33-year-old Chris Farley died on December 18, 1997, he was hailed as a comic genius. But what were the same folk saying about *Beverly Hills Ninja* when Farley was alive?

Most people, perhaps even Farley himself, anticipated his early death. Friends say he idolized John Belushi, even to the point of admiring Belushi's premature demise. That's taking hero worship a bit far.

One of Farley's most well-known *SNL* characters was of the Chicago Superfan. During a Bears call-in show, his character inevitably had multiple heart attacks but always revived himself through self-administered CPR. That's pretty much how the real Farley died, according to the coroner, with one main difference: he forgot to administer CPR. Farley's brother found the 300-pound actor in the front foyer of his condominium, right where a stripper admitted leaving him after a long night of partying.

Hancock Center, 60th Floor, 125 E. Delaware Pl., Chicago, IL 60611

Hours: Private residence, never open; view from outside

Cost: Free

Directions: Just north of Water Tower Place.

Eugene Izzi Death Site

Eugene Izzi was a mystery writer whose death was as puzzling as his crime novels. Police found Izzi hanging from his 14th-floor office balcony on the morning of December 7, 1996. Izzi was being treated for depression and his office door was locked from the inside, so police ruled his death a suicide. But was it?

The author was found wearing a bulletproof vest and had three computer disks in his pocket. On the disks were 800 pages of a crime story that paralleled his own murder, suicide, or accidental death—whatever it was. In the outline, members of an Indiana militia try to kill an author by hanging him out the window of his 14th-floor office. Friends of Izzi claim he was a stickler for details and might have been trying out one of his plot twists when the experiment went horribly wrong. Or was it an Indiana militia? Izzi had been telling his friends that a group was after him because of his research on the new novel.

Or perhaps the guy wanted folks to talk about him after his death, which is just what people are doing. You be the judge.

Tower Building, 6 N. Michigan Ave., Room 1418, Chicago, IL 60602

Hours: Always visible; view from outside

Cost: Free

Directions: At Madison and Michigan Aves.

DEAD IN LINCOLN PARK

Chicago's Lincoln Park is a peaceful place, but at one time it was a rest-in-peace place—it was the city cemetery! The graveyard extended from North Avenue to Armitage, and from Clark to Lake Michigan. In 1859, the city began moving bodies to newer, outlying cemeteries like Graceland and Rosehill. But crews didn't get all the bodies. You can still find graves today.

For example, the tomb of Ira Couch still stands just behind the Chicago Historical Society. Neither the funds nor the permission were ever available to move the 100-ton mausoleum. Nobody is quite sure how many bodies are in the lonely monument today.

Early Chicago native David Kennison is also buried in Lincoln Park, closer to the Zoo. Kennison claimed to have participated in the Boston Tea Party, the Battle of Bunker Hill, and the Fort Dearborn Massacre. For his stories to have been accurate, he would have had to have been 115 years old when he died in 1852, hardly believable to anyone but the DAR. The organization erected an engraved boulder to Kennison near the Academy of Sciences building.

There are many unmarked bodies still left in the park, too. Fifteen bodies were unearthed in 1986 during construction near the Chicago Historical Society, and fragments of six more were discovered while excavating the museum's new parking garage in 1998. So if your dog fetches a bone during a walk through the park, take a good look at it. It might be older than you think.

Clarence Darrow's Ashes

Before Clarence Darrow died on March 13, 1938, he made a promise to his friends: he claimed he would return to them on the anniversary of his death if there was an afterlife. If he didn't, they could safely assume they too would be food for worms. His ashes were scattered over Wooded Island in the Jackson Park Lagoon, adjacent to a bridge that today bears his name.

Each year, people gather at the bridge on March 13, but Darrow never shows up. However, some people claim to have seen his ghost from the bridge at night, standing on the back steps to the Museum of Science and Industry. Witnesses admit the figure is nondescript and stays hundreds of feet away, so until the specter clears up, the agnostic lawyer has yet to speak from beyond.

Jackson Park, Clarence Darrow Bridge, 5900 S. Lake Shore Dr., Chicago, IL 60637

Hours: Always visible

Cost: Free

Directions: The bridge crosses the lagoon at about 59th St.

Oak Woods Cemetery

Oak Woods is one of the South Side's largest and most beautiful cemeteries. It is the final resting place for Jesse Owens, Harold Washington, "Big Jim" Colosimo, Ida B. Wells, and thousands of Confederate prisoners.

Jesse Owens won four gold medals and broke three world records at the 1936 Berlin Olympics, much to Adolph Hitler's dismay. You'd think a star athlete would stay away from cigarettes. He didn't and died of lung cancer in 1980. His gravesite overlooks the small lake to the west of the main entrance.

Chicago Mayor Harold Washington was buried in Oak Woods after his lifelong attachment to food got the better of him. Every week since his death, a red rose has appeared on his grave. Washington is buried in a gray granite mausoleum southwest of the main gate.

Behind Washington is a tall obelisk marking the grave of "Big Jim" Colosimo, Al Capone's Mob predecessor. In a hit planned by Little John Torrio, Colosimo was gunned down on May 11, 1920.

Civil rights leader Ida B. Wells, a journalist who documented lynchings of African Americans throughout the United States, is also buried in Oak Woods. She died in 1931.

Finally, about 6,000 Confederate prisoners who died at Camp Douglas, only 4,200 of whom were "official," are buried in Oak Woods under the Confederate Monument in the southwest corner of the cemetery. When you stand atop the mound, you are standing over thousands of Rebel bodies laid out in radiating concentric circles.

1035 E. 67th St., Chicago, IL 60637

(773) 288-3800

Hours: Daily 9A.M.–5P.M.

Cost: Free

Directions: Bounded by 67th and 71st Sts., between Cottage Grove and the Illinois Central railroad tracks; enter from 67th St.

Bohemian National Cemetery

Further down on the Chicago cemetery ladder is Bohemian National. You used to have to be Czech to be planted here, but the ethnic restriction has been lifted. What it lacks in famous residents it makes up for in cool headstones and monuments. You won't find a larger collection of angels, cherubic dead babies, and soldiers anywhere in the Windy City.

Bohemian contains perhaps the spookiest monument in all of the Chicago area. It was created by Albin Polasek for the Stejskal-Buchal crypt and is a hooded old hag coming to claim the souls of the people interred within. Rest in peace? Not likely!

5255 N. Pulaski, Chicago, IL 60630

(773) 539-8442

Hours: Daily 9A.M.–5P.M.

Cost: Free

Directions: At the corner of Pulaski and Foster.

SHANE LESLIE
"Chicago has all the possibilities of becoming the earth's final city, the Babylon of the Plains."

JOHN L. PEYTON
"The city is situated on both sides of the Chicago River, a sluggish, slimy stream, too lazy to clean itself . . ."

Another superstition debunked.

Graceland Cemetery

As cemeteries go, Graceland is drop-dead gorgeous. It's the perfect place for a picnic, though that's not exactly encouraged. Some of Chicago's best-known citizens are planted at this cemetery, but three lesser-known residents get most of the attention these days, at least from ghost lovers: Inez Clark, Ludwig Wolff, and Dexter Graves.

Inez Clark died in 1880 at a young age from tuberculosis. Her parents were overcome with grief, so they marked her grave with a life-sized replica of the girl sitting on a bench. They could then see her angelic face whenever they visited. To protect it from the pigeons, they encased the statue in glass. It may keep out the birds, but the case isn't strong enough to hold Inez's spirit. Her statue is said to cry real tears and run around the tombstones at night while the bench and box sit empty, filled only with a slight mist. This event usually takes place on August 1. If you live in the area, expect a heavy police presence around Graceland's perimeter to discourage devil-worshippers.

Ludwig Wolff, unlike Inez, is entombed in an underground mausoleum and cannot escape. Apparently he's not too happy about it, because people have heard him howling from inside his granite tomb. Others claim it isn't Wolff, but a green-eyed ghost dog who lives inside and protects his dead master. Either way, would you want to find out?

Graceland's scariest monument is the hooded figure over Dexter Graves's plot dubbed "Eternal Silence," carved by Lorado Taft in 1909. It has also been called "The Statue of Death." It is said to be impossible to photograph, but as you can see above, that's not true.

4001 N. Clark St., Chicago, IL 60613

(773) 525-1105

Hours: Daily 8A.M.–5P.M.

Cost: Free

Directions: Enter from Irving Park Rd. and Clark St.; Clark is along the road to the left; Wolff is along the north wall; Graves is east of the crematorium.

ALSO PLANTED IN GRACELAND

Daniel Burnham Chicago's city planner had his ashes planted on an island on Lake Willomere in the northeast corner of the cemetery.

Marshall Field The mercantile genius rests beneath a seated figure atop a platform, called "Memory." The statue was an early inspiration for the Lincoln Memorial in Washington, D.C. Both were done by Daniel Chester French and Henry Bacon. Field died January 1, 1906, of pneumonia contracted while playing golf in December.

William A. Hulbert Baseball's first National League president is buried beneath a giant granite baseball with the league's first eight cities etched upon it.

John Kinzie The first European settler to the area, he survived the Fort Dearborn Massacre of 1812 when 52 settlers were killed near 1600 S. Indiana Ave. This is Kinzie's fourth resting place.

Cyrus McCormick The Inventor of the Harvesting Machine was planted here after he was harvested by the Grim Reaper.

Walter Newberry Founder of the Newberry Library, he died overseas and was shipped back to Chicago in a barrel of rum. He was buried here in the same barrel.

Potter and Bertha Honoré Palmer Developer of State Street and focal point of High Society, they've got the snazziest sarcophagi in the cemetery. Part of *Damien, Omen II* was filmed near the Palmers.

Allan Pinkerton Founder of the Secret Service, Pinkerton became the nation's first private eye after botching the Lincoln job. Several of his faithful employees, one of whom was killed pursuing Jesse James, are buried by his side.

George Pullman Sleeping car magnate and union buster, interred in a lead-lined casket in a cement vault beneath steel railroad tracks (and more cement). These precautions were to deter graverobbers and angry former employees. Rumors have long circulated that he was actually preserved in formaldehyde in the basement of his Pullman mansion, but the odds are he's here, and NOBODY is getting him out.

Louis Sullivan The influential architect died penniless. His monument was placed here years after his death by admirers and includes two half-profiles of skyscrapers on the sides. Sullivan designed the Getty Tomb in Graceland, called "a symphony in stone" by Frank Lloyd Wright.

Ludwig Mies van der Rohe Architect of the glass box skyscraper who stated, "Less is more."

Rosehill Cemetery

Rosehill is no Graceland in terms of beauty, celebrities, or spooks, but it's a close second. If acreage is anything, Rosehill is the city's largest boneyard.

Filed away in Rosehill's large Mausoleum, retailers Montgomery Ward and Richard Sears are locked together in eternal combat. They didn't get along in life any better than they seem to in death. Late-night visitors have spotted Sears's ghost stepping out of his tomb and moving toward Ward's crypt . . . and nobody believes he's bargain hunting.

The ghosts of Frances Pearce and her infant daughter are less famous than Sears, but more disturbing. After they died during childbirth in 1864, Pearce's husband, Horatio Stone, commissioned a "sleeping" statue of the pair to be placed in a glass case over their graves. Each year in May, on the anniversary of their deaths, the box is said to fill with a white mist and the two statues sit up to say hello to visitors . . . who run away screaming.

Rosehill has many weird monuments which, if they aren't haunted already, should be. Life-sized renderings of Charles Hull (namesake of Hull House) and Leonard Volk (sculptor of both Lincoln and Douglas) sit comfortably in chairs atop their respective graves. George Bangs has a three-foot railroad car entering a tunnel for his monument; Bangs perfected the mail car while head of the Railway Mail Service.

A couple of spurned lovers round out the odd monuments. A 10-foot phallus was erected over the grave of Lillian Jenkins by her jilted ex-husband, S. A. Jennings. Jenkins divorced Jennings after finding him in an affair, and this is how he repaid her. Lifelong bachelor Charles DuPluesses's monument reads, "Now Ain't That Too Bad." He went to his grave believing women should have paid him more attention.

5800 N. Ravenswood, Chicago, IL 60660

(773) 561-5940

Hours: Daily 9A.M.–5P.M.; tours first and third Saturday of each month at 10A.M.

Cost: Free

Directions: Just south of Peterson, between Western and Ravenswood.

Camp Douglas and the Douglas Tomb

Lincoln's Democratic contender, Steven A. Douglas, died on June 3, 1861,
shortly after the Civil War began. His body was interred on his Oakenwald
estate south of downtown.

It is hard to imagine he got much rest because the Union built a prison
camp in Oakenwald's backyard, naming it in his honor: Camp Douglas.
Conditions in the stockade bound by Cottage Grove, Giles, 31st and 33rd
Streets were nothing short of deplorable. Of the 30,000 Confederate troops
imprisoned here from 1862 to 1865, 6,129 died. Most were buried in Oak
Woods Cemetery.

After the war, a fitting monument to Douglas was planned. During
its construction, for two years during the late 1860s, the public could
view Douglas through the glass-topped lid of his sarcophagus. He has
since been shielded from the elements and the lookie-loos. Too bad. The
statue atop the 96-foot-tall monument is 9 feet 9 inches tall, almost twice
the height of the man for which it was fashioned.

Stephen A. Douglas Tomb, 636 E. 35th St., Chicago, IL 60616

(312) 225-2620

Hours: Daily 9A.M.–5P.M.

Cost: Free

www.state.il.us/hpa/DOUGT.HTM

Directions: At Cottage Grove Ave. at the end of 35th St., across from Ellis Park.

Coming in for that final landing.

O'Hare's Cemeteries

It's rather unsettling to see a cemetery just outside your window when landing at O'Hare International, but if you come in on the airport's southernmost east-west runway, that's what you'll see. It's St. Johannes and its sister Resthaven, the two oldest cemeteries in the city limits. They were established long before the Wright Brothers. When Orchard Field opened, they stood their ground. Orchard became O'Hare, and the dead never moved.

If you like to watch airplanes landing, St. Johannes Cemetery is a perfect location, assuming they're landing on that runway. The graveyard is wedged between the landing strip and the Federal Express hanger; all you have to do is check in at the trailer on the dirt road.

Resthaven Cemetery and St. Johannes Cemetery, Chicago, IL 60666

Hours: Summer 11A.M.–5P.M.; winter 10A.M.–3P.M.

Cost: Free

Directions: West on Irving Park Rd. from Mannheim Rd., north on the dirt road just after you pass under the railroad tracks.

Day of the Dead

With all this talk of death, you might feel depressed. So stop on by the Mexican Fine Arts Center in October for their annual Day of the Dead show. That ought to cheer you up! Their exhibition is said to be the nation's largest of its kind and includes many elaborate memorial altars created by Chicago artists, decorated sugar skulls, tissue paper cutout demonstrations, and more.

Mexican Fine Arts Center, 1852 W. 19th St., Chicago, IL 60608

(773) 738-1503

Hours: Tuesday–Sunday 10A.M.–5P.M.

Cost: Free

Directions: Two blocks west of Ashland, four blocks north of Cermak, on the south side of Harrison Park.

CHICAGO SUBURBS

*M*any people see the suburbs as dull, featureless nowhere-villes, hardly worth visiting on valuable vacation time, and for the most part, they're right. But there are a few spots in the Chicago suburbs where you can enjoy yourself and give people the idea you actually went someplace exotic. All you need is a camera and the ability to lie through your teeth.

Get a shot of yourself toasting with a tropical drink at the Hala Kahiki. Tell everyone you went to Hawaii. Pose in front of the Leaning Tower of Niles. Instant Italy! The Tropic World exhibit at the Brookfield Zoo can double as the Amazon rainforest or the jungles of Cameroon. Your friends will either be impressed or think you're a freak.

An eight-car pileup.

Berwyn
Art Mall

If you don't think of art when you think of a mall, perhaps you should visit Cermak Plaza. This shopping center commissioned artists to spruce up the place, and what they created has been upsetting the locals ever since.

The largest piece is called "The Spindle." Creator Dustin Shuler skewered eight automobiles on a giant nail in the middle of the parking lot. Along the sidewalk are 20 other visual- and sound-related sculptures in various stages of disrepair, including "Pinto Pelt" (also by Shuler), the skinned gold shell of the flammable Ford. While the pieces may not be as stunning as when they were originally installed, there's enough to keep you entertained.

Critics have long complained that "The Spindle" attracts pigeons, but they have quieted somewhat since the work appeared in *Wayne's World*. And if the Berwyn police have any input, it will never come down; they use the mall to haze new recruits. Dispatchers send rookies out to the plaza to investigate an "eight-car pileup."

Cermak Plaza, 7043 Cermak Rd., Berwyn, IL 60402

(708) 344-9242

Hours: Always visible

Cost: Free

Directions: At Cermak and Harlem Aves.

Brookfield
Binti-Jua, Mother of the Year

On August 16, 1996, a three-year-old boy crawled over a guardrail and planter box to get a better look at the critters in Brookfield Zoo's Tropic World. He got it, falling 24 feet into a pit filled with gorillas. Luckily for him, one gorilla, Binti-Jua, was a recent mother who had been trained to be nurturing by her human jailers. She picked up the unconscious child and dragged him 40 feet to an outside gate. Meanwhile, zookeepers were hosing down the other gorillas to keep them away.

In Illinois, monkeys have done time for shoplifting, so it was encouraging to hear news that one of our primate relatives had done something positive. Newt Gingrich seized the opportunity to observe that Binti-Jua was more nurturing than some welfare mothers and was rightfully criticized. Binti-Jua was proclaimed Mother of the Year and received worldwide attention. She even got a rhinestone pendant from the American Legion. Nobody seemed to entertain the notion that perhaps she dragged the child over to the door in exchange for a banana.

Brookfield Zoo, 3300 Golf Rd., Brookfield, IL 60513

(708) 485-0263

Hours: Daily 10A.M.–4:30P.M.; summers to 5:30P.M.

Cost: Adults $6, Seniors(65+) $3, Kids(3–11) $3, October–March, Tuesdays and Thursdays free

www.brookfieldzoo.org

Directions: At First Ave. and 31st St.

Darien
National Shrine of St. Therese
Museum and Gift Shop

Relic lovers know the problem: if you want to see the bone chip of a saint you usually have to catch a church when it's open, and that means getting up early on a Sunday morning. But at the National Shrine of St. Therese, you can stop by whenever's convenient.

The relics on display here are only those of St. Therese of Lisieux, but they've got some good ones. The best? "A particle of St. Therese's uncorrupted flesh, discovered when her decomposed body was exhumed in the municipal cemetery of Lisieux, September 6, 1910." Was she uncorrupted, or decomposed? The placard seems to want it both ways.

But that flesh blob isn't all. They've got bone chips, locks of hair, her toy tambourine, prayer books, and a chair from her cell in a French convent. There are also plenty of spooky statues and the Largest Religious Wood Carving in the United States, a tableau of St. Therese's life.

Carmelite Visitors Center, 8501 Bailey Rd., Darien, IL 60561

(630) 969-3311

Hours: Daily 10A.M.–4P.M.

Cost: Free

www.saint-therese.org

Directions: Cass Ave. Exit from I-55, north to Frontage Rd., west to Bailey Rd.

Des Plaines
The First McDonald's

To call this ex-restaurant/museum "The First McDonald's" is more than misleading. The first McDonald's Restaurant was located in San Bernadino, California, and was run by Maurice and Richard McDonald. But the brothers' Multimixer salesman, Ray Kroc, bought the right to franchise their operation in 1954, and that is where the modern corporation's revisionist history begins. On April 15, 1955, Ray Kroc opened the Des Plaines McDonald's, and it was a huge success. By 1960, Kroc bought the McDonalds' entire operation for $2.7 million, then proceeded to run them out of business. They weren't even allowed to continue using their own last name.

Today, only the sign in front of the museum is original. The restaurant was torn down, then rebuilt for burger-loving tourists. Look through its windows at wax dummies serving plastic food to nonexistent customers. Visit the basement museum and learn about the early sexist policy of refusing to hire women. (They relented in 1968, but the 1960s were a crazy time!) And reflect on how much has changed from the company's early years; a manager's handbook once directed, "Personnel with bad teeth, severe skin blemishes, or tattoos should not be stationed at service windows." How things have changed!

McDonald's #1 Store Museum, 400 N. Lee St., Des Plaines, IL 60016

(847) 297-5022

Hours: May–September, Thursday–Saturday 10:30A.M.–2:30P.M.

Cost: Free

Directions: Just north of where Lee/Mannheim Rd. crosses the downtown railroad tracks.

Breakfast on a train.

The Choo-Choo Restaurant

Just two blocks from McDonald's monument to restaurant homogeneity stands a burger joint with real character. The Choo-Choo Restaurant draws its name from its method of presentation. Your order is taken by a waitress but delivered by a toy train! Plastic plates straddle flatbed cars that ride on a track from the kitchen. Only the stools and booths around the central island receive train service, so come during off-peak hours if you want your hamburger on a choo-choo.

Be sure to saddle up in the corner on a still-operating mechanical pony. For 10¢ you can pretend you're Roy Rogers or Dale Evans.

600 N. Lee St., Des Plaines, IL 60016

(847) 298-5949

Hours: Saturday–Thursday 6A.M.–5P.M., Friday 6A.M.–8P.M.

Cost: Meals $3–$6

Directions: Two blocks south of the McDonald's Museum, just north of Miner.

Elmhurst
American Movie Palace Museum

The Theatre Historical Society of America is dedicated to cataloging and preserving theater buildings regardless of their primary usage, be they for movies, opera, dancing, theater, nickelodeons, or vaudeville. While the archives occupy more space than the exhibits, the museum does have an impressive collection of artifacts from many now-leveled movie palaces.

By far the most impressive display is a scale model of the interior of Chicago's 1927 Avalon Theatre (now known as the New Regal Theatre). The Avalon Video Theatre was constructed over three years by THSA member Frank Cronican. The former set builder paid close attention to detail, down to the exact paint shades from the original structure. Plaster lions on chains crouch on the balconies, fake trees pop up on the horizon, and a large video screen rests on the stage. The THSA will soon make the Avalon Video Theatre a permanent exhibit, complete with cloud and star projectors for the ceiling.

Also on display are architectural remnants of many famous theaters, such as an arch finial and a house phone from New York's demolished Roxy. You can see Radio City Music Hall's Wurlitzer Organ reproduced in miniature by Robert Longfield. They've also got "exit" signs, ushers' uniforms, velvety seats, and lighting fixtures from across the nation.

Theatre Historical Society of America, 152 N. York St., Suite 200, Elmhurst, IL 60126

(630) 782-1800

E-mail: thrhistsoc@aol.com

Hours: Monday–Wednesday, Friday 9A.M.–4P.M., Thursday 10A.M.–3P.M.

Cost: Donations encouraged

www2.hawaii.edu/~angell/thsa/

Directions: Just north of the York Theater entrance.

DES PLAINES
Baseball announcer **Harry Caray** was laid to rest in All Saints Cemetery (700 N. River Rd.) in Des Plaines under a headstone that reads "Holy Cow!"

ELMHURST
Labor leader **Eugene Debs** died in Elmhurst on November 20, 1926.

Lizzadro Museum of Lapidary Art

What is "lapidary art"? This museum's brochure defines it best: "Lapidary art combines the miracles of nature, the mysteries of science, and the creative genius of man in the medium of stone." About the only places you still see lapidary art practiced in abundance are in onyx chess sets and jade figurines, both of which are decorating no-no's.

The museum began as the personal collection of master carver Joseph F. Lizzadro (1898–1972). Many of the pieces were done by Lizzadro himself. Though the world's largest collection of carved Chinese jade is impressive, the best pieces are the small dioramas along the outer wall of the museum. Look closely for the animal figures made of semiprecious stones: a barnyard with glassy pink pigs, Iggy the Elephant out for a walk (carved partly with the real dead Iggy's tusks!), the "Age of Dinosaurs" with species from conflicting geologic eras, and a herd of buffalo on the Great Prairie.

220 Cottage Hill Ave., Elmhurst, IL 60126

(630) 833-1616

Hours: Tuesday–Saturday 10A.M.–5P.M., Sunday 1–5P.M.

Cost: Adults $2.50, Seniors(60+) $1.50, Kids $1, Fridays free

www.elmhurst.org/LIZZMUS.HTM

Directions: In Wilder Park, three blocks north of St. Charles Rd. and two blocks west of York Rd.

Evanston
Rest Cottage and the WCTU Headquarters

In the U.S. Capitol's Statuary Hall, each state has chosen one native son or daughter to represent it. Illinois has chosen Frances Willard, a woman barely known today to most in this state. But in her day, Willard was a monumental figure.

Frances Willard was the Women's Christian Temperance Union's second president, from 1879 to 1898, and its most influential. She wrote and promoted the Polyglot Petition in 1885, asking Congress to outlaw alcohol, opium, and tobacco. Though 7.5 million people signed it worldwide, the petition didn't have any immediate effect except to demonstrate the political muscle of active women. Willard died in 1898, years before women's suffrage and Prohibition, but both constitutional amendments can be strongly attributed to her efforts and those of the WCTU.

Willard lived in an 1865 Victorian home built for her father near Northwestern University and dubbed "Rest Cottage" by her mother. The home appears much as it did when Willard lived there, preserved by her companion and secretary, Anna Gordon. Family mementos and WCTU artifacts fill this large but comfortable home, including a begonia propagated from one first potted by Willard. You'll see rolls of the Polyglot Petition, the family Bible signed with each member's temperance pledge, dolls representing each Willard family member, and a huge bell cast from 1,000 confiscated opium and tobacco pipes.

Rest Cottage, 1730 Chicago Ave., Evanston, IL 60201

(847) 864-1396

Hours: March–December, first Sunday of every month, 1–4P.M.

Cost: Adults $3

www.wctu.org

Directions: One block north of Dempster.

Another soul to be saved.

Prehistoric Life Museum

Tucked away in the basement of a quiet Evanston rock shop is a remarkable collection of prehistoric creatures. Arranged in order by geologic age, these 1,000+ specimens are the collection of Dave and Sandra Douglass, along with a few pieces from their family and friends.

Dave started collecting fossils when he was in high school and has made some amazing discoveries over the years. One fossil, a giant scorpion, was named *Titanoscorpio Douglassi* in his honor. His parents caught the rockhound bug, and they too discovered new extinct species; his father found a dragonfly nymph (*Mischoptera Douglassi*) that filled a gap in dragonfly evolution, and his mother unearthed the oldest known fossilized squid (*Jeletka Douglassae*).

The Douglass's specimens are attractively displayed, still embedded in rock but cleaned so as to be easily examined. Most of the critters are creepy and unfamiliar, like the Tully Monster, Illinois's state fossil. *Tullimonstrum Gregarium* was a one-foot, tubelike invertebrate that lived from 280 to 340 million years ago in the Illinois Sea. The Tully Monster had two paddle eyes that scientists have not yet been able to explain.

They've also got a fair share of dinosaur samples, both footprints and bones, and a makeshift cave for dramatic effect. For the money, this place beats the Field Museum hands down, and that would be the case even if it wasn't free.

Dave's Down to Earth Rock Shop, 704 Main St., Evanston, IL 60202

(847) 866-7374

Hours: Monday–Tuesday, Thursday–Friday 10:30A.M.–5:30P.M., Saturday 10A.M.–5P.M.

Cost: Free

Directions: One block west of Chicago Ave.

EVANSTON

The ghost of a Lake Michigan drowning victim has been spotted running across Sheridan Road from the shore into Calvary Cemetery (301 Chicago), anxious to find a warm, dry grave.

Actors **William Christopher** (October 20, 1932), **Barbara Harris** (July 25, 1935), **Elizabeth McGovern** (July 18, 1961), **Joan Cusack** (October 11, 1962), and **John Cusack** (June 28, 1966) were all born in Evanston.

The **Unabomber's** first bomb exploded at Northwestern University's Technological Institute in Evanston on May 26, 1978, injuring a campus security guard. His second bomb also targeted the Institute. On May 9, 1979, a cigar-box device injured a civil engineering graduate student.

Unless there is a fire, it is illegal to change clothes in a car without drapes in Evanston.

Forest Park
Haymarket Martyrs Monument and Emma Goldman's Grave

The four men executed for the Haymarket Riot, and the one who committed suicide before his hanging, were not allowed to be buried within the Chicago city limits, so their bodies were laid to rest just across the city's border in Forest Park. Their three pardoned comrades were also buried here after they died, as were part of Wobblie Joe Hill's ashes and Anarchist Emma Goldman. This "Dissenter's Row" is sometimes called "The Communist Plot."

A monument to the Haymarket martyrs was erected and dedicated in 1893 and has been the location of many labor rallies since. Every year on the Sunday closest to May 4 you can join the Black Sunday gathering for long speeches to small crowds.

Forest Home Cemetery was built on an old Indian burial ground and bones have been unearthed when graves have been opened, so be wary of poltergeist activity. To spook yourself, check out the monument erected by the United Ancient Order of Druids. There are three concentric rings around a central monument topped by a guy looking like Willie Nelson. He carries a walking stick on which is carved the head of a child. Spooky! You can also find monuments to the International Alliance of Bill Posters and Billers, the Cigar Makers International Union, and the Independent Order of Odd Fellows.

Forest Home (Waldheim) Cemetery, 863 S. Des Plaines Ave., Forest Park, IL 60130

(708) 366-1900

Hours: Daily 9A.M.–5P.M.

Cost: Free

sunsite.berkeley.edu/Goldman/

Directions: Three blocks north of Roosevelt Rd., 11 blocks west of Harlem Ave.

ALSO PLANTED IN FOREST HOME

Dr. Clarence and Grace Hall Hemingway Ernest Hemingway's parents; Dr. Hemingway shot himself with a Civil War pistol.

Mike Todd Elizabeth Taylor's husband, who directed *Around the World in 80 Days* and perished in a plane crash, is buried here.

Need a lift?

Justice
Resurrection Mary

Ghost stories of phantom hitchhikers are not uncommon, but perhaps the best one is that of Resurrection Mary. Her tale goes something like this: A lonely guy driving along Archer Avenue at night comes across a beautiful blond young woman in a white dress. She asks for a ride home, sometimes after they go to a dance, then leads him to the gates of Resurrection Cemetery. She hops out of the car, runs toward the gate, and vanishes. During the night the driver had learned Mary's mother's address and goes to visit her, only to discover that Mary was killed years ago driving home from a dance at the Oh Henry (now Willowbrook) Ballroom.

Resurrection Mary was first spotted in 1939, and the stories of encounters remained fairly consistent. Then, during the 1960s and 1970s, Mary took on a more political agenda. She not only wanted a ride back to her grave, but to warn the human population about the end of the world, including the Second Coming of Christ. In 1977, she vandalized the gates to the cemetery, this time trying to get out. A witness spotted her glowing figure inside the gate, pulling on the bars. Some claim you could see her hand prints embedded into the metal, but the bars have since been removed, or bent back with a welding torch, depending on whom you ask.

Many have speculated as to which Mary in the cemetery she is, but because there are so many young, dead Marys at Resurrection, there is a disagreement. Top contenders are Mary Bregovy (Section MM, site 9819) and

Mary Duranski, both of whom died in 1934 in car crashes coming home from dances. If you happen to run into her, be sure to ask her full name so this can be cleared up.

Resurrection Cemetery, 7200 S. Archer Ave., Justice, IL 60458

(708) 458-4770

Hours: Daily 9A.M.–5P.M.

Cost: Free

Directions: Cemetery is bound by Archer Ave. (Rte. 171), 79th St., and Roberts Rd.

Lansing
First Lady Dolls

If you can't make it to the Smithsonian to see the real inaugural gowns of the First Ladies, perhaps this little museum will do you. Each inaugural gown has been reproduced and placed on foot-tall dolls by Sophie Drolenga. Many have two-inch plastic husbands by their sides.

You'll notice that the First Ladies' faces are identical; only their hair color and clothing changes. The only exceptions are Barbara Bush and Hillary Clinton, both of whose faces are hideously bloated. It works for Barbara, not for Hillary.

The rest of this museum is filled with the standard historical society fare: spinning wheels, quilts, old plates, mementos from the Columbian Exposition, and stuffed dead animals.

Lansing Historical Society & Museum, 2750 Indiana Ave., PO Box 1776, Lansing, IL 60438

(708) 474-6160

Hours: Monday 6–8P.M., Wednesday 3–5P.M., Saturday 10A.M.–Noon

Cost: Donations encouraged

Directions: In the basement of the Lewis O. Flom Lansing Public Library.

LEMONT

Radio commentator **Paul Harvey** was busted for trespassing at the Argonne National Laboratory in Lemont in 1951 in a stunt aimed at pointing out the facility's poor security.

Don't be fooled by the **Mother Theresa Museum** in Lemont (14700 Main). This isn't the Mother Theresa we all knew, but another: Mother Mary Theresa Dudzik, a Franciscan Sister.

Lemont
Ghost Monks

St. James of the Sag is Cook County's oldest church, and its most haunted. Parishioners should have expected as much, building on the site of an Indian burial ground! When the church basement was excavated in the 1830s, workers uncovered Native American bones but continued building the church anyway. The parish was mostly made up of Irish immigrants, many of whom died early, ghastly deaths while working on the nearby Sanitary and Ship Canal.

It isn't the canal workers who haunt the grounds, but instead a group of ghost monks. They were first sighted floating along the ridge near the church in 1847, and as the cemetery filled up around the chapel, more monks were reported. Witnesses often claimed to hear them chanting in Latin. The most recent sighting occurred in November 1977 when policemen chased seven monks up the hill after receiving a report of intruders in the graveyard after dark. When the monks reached the peak, they disappeared.

A more ominous specter associated with St. James of the Sag is a horse-drawn hearse spotted along Archer Ave. The driverless carriage races through the night, horses frothing, with a baby's glowing casket seen through the viewing window.

St. James of the Sag Church, 10600 Archer Ave., Lemont, IL 60439

(630) 257-7000

Hours: Daily 9A.M.–5P.M.

Cost: Free

Directions: Northeast of town, just east of the Rte. 83, 107th St., and Rte. 171 intersection.

Lincolnwood
Novelty Golf and the Bunny Hutch

This 50-year-old miniature golf course could never be accused of being the slickest course around, but perhaps the one with the most character. Suburban minature golf courses tend to be polished, prefab enterprises, but Novelty Golf looks like it's been slapped together with objects from every-where. Mismatched statues appear to have had previous lives as business advertisements, the buildings look like they were built in a junior high shop class, and there is nothing that even remotely resembles a theme. Over the two 18-hole courses you'll see tiki heads, the Hancock Tower, an out-of-water mermaid, and the scariest looking Humpty Dumpty on the planet.

Adjacent to Novelty Golf you'll find the Bunny Hutch, a classic burger shack. They don't serve bunny burgers, so tell the kids not to worry. Guarding the hutch is another fiberglass creature, but this one looks like Bugs Bunny on speed.

3650 W. Devon Ave., Lincolnwood, IL 60659

(847) 679-9434

Hours: April–October 10A.M.–Midnight

Cost: Before 6P.M. $4, after 6P.M. $6

Directions: At the corner of Devon and Lincoln Aves.

How *not* to fake a ghost photograph.

Midlothian
Bachelor's Grove Cemetery

Most Chicago-area spook experts agree: Bachelor's Grove Cemetery is the most haunted spot in the area. The cemetery was established during the Blackhawk Wars; few people have been buried there since the 1940s. It fell into disrepair and was vandalized by bored teenagers and beer-guzzling boneheads. Tombstones were kicked over and spray painted. Caskets were pulled from the ground. House pets were sacrificed.

Bachelor's Grove's "residents" reacted with an all-out effort to scare off the intruders. People began seeing floating blue lights, misty figures, faces on tombstones, unexplainable cold spots, red streaks through the sky along the road. Others spotted the ghost of an unfortunate farmer whose jittery horse pulled them both into a nearby swamp to drown. A two-headed man was once seen rising from the same swamp, crawling toward the highway. Ghost sedans raced along the turnpike where gangsters dumped bodies. A phantom farmhouse appeared along the dirt road, but faded into the distance whenever anyone approached it. And on full moons, the Madonna of Bachelor's Grove (also known as Mrs. Rogers) walked the haunted ground in a white gown with a dead baby ghost in her arms.

Sadly, there isn't much left to see these days, but you'll probably run into somebody looking for ghosts if not the ghosts themselves. Police guard the place on Halloween, though on most nights it's easy to sneak onto the property... not that you should. But bring a camera if you do, just in case...

Bachelor's Grove in Rubio Woods, 6000 W. Midlothian Turnpike (143rd St.), Midlothian, IL 60445

Hours: Daily 9A.M.–5P.M.

Cost: Free

www.students.uiuc.edu/~g-jaros/ghost/grove.html

Directions: On the south side of the road, across from the soccer fields east of Ridgeland Ave. down the abandoned road.

Morton Grove
Par King

When you step onto the Par King miniature golf course, you'll think you stepped through a time warp. This attraction was built in 1964, and nothing seems to have changed since opening day. The design features are freshly painted, the hedges are neatly trimmed. One hole has a replica of One Prudential Plaza, the tallest Chicago skyscraper when Par King opened, and there are no holes based upon the lunar landing or *The Little Mermaid*.

The best shot at Par King is the Roller Coaster hole. If you can putt into the coaster's "loading area," your ball goes on a journey around an old fashioned wooden coaster before being dumped near the final hole.

And for you grown-up miniature golf aficionados, Par King has evening hours for adults and high schoolers only. This doesn't mean you're allowed to curse like a truck driver when you blow a putt, but you will be able to finish a round in short order.

6711 Dempster, Morton Grove, IL 60053

(847) 965-3333

Hours: Summers 10:30A.M.–7:30P.M.; adults only 7:30–10P.M.

Cost: Days Monday–Friday $5, Saturday–Sunday $5.50; Evenings Monday–Friday $5, Saturday–Sunday $6

Directions: Three blocks east of Waukegan Rd. on Dempster.

This mistake was planned.

Niles
Tower of Pisa

Why go to Europe to see the Tower of Pisa when there's one right here? This half-scale replica of the Italian blunder is a cleverly disguised water tower and works just fine for photos. It was built in 1933 to supply water to the three swimming pools of industrialist Robert Ilg. Architect Albert Farr was criticized for building a heavy, tilted structure—some dubbed it Farr's Folly—but it has withstood the test of time and could outlast its namesake.

Today the 96-foot-tall structure serves as an attention-getter for the YMCA, but is no longer filled with water. A park was built around its base, complete with a Leaning Telefono Booth of Niles.

Leaning Tower YMCA

6300 W. Touhy Ave., Niles, IL 60714

(847) 647-8222

Hours: Always visible

Cost: Free

Directions: Two blocks east of N. Caldwell Ave.

Oak Brook
The Ray Kroc Museum

Judging from this museum's nonexistent advertising and its weekday-only hours, the Ray Kroc Museum is intended more for the prospective franchisee than the general public. But if you can find the time, you're welcome to visit. Located on the ground floor of McDonald's corporate headquarters, accessed through a McStore gift shop, the Ray Kroc Museum is a tribute to the tireless enterprise of one man, a man so driven he once said of his competitors, "If they were drowning to death, I'd put a hose in their mouths."

Yes, you'll follow Ray's exploits when he first sold paper cups for Lily, how the flat-bottomed paper cup revolutionized the industry, and how the Multimixer Years (1940 to 1954) led him to the McDonald brothers and his eventual fortune. A multimedia presentation and mechanical diorama show how the greasy, character-filled diners of yesteryear were transformed into the sanitary, bland food factories of today. Final thoughts are offered by the sanitary, bland, blather-factory George Will.

There are plenty of things to learn about Kroc and McDonald's that you might not have known, like how Ray was in the same American Red Cross company during World War I as Walt Disney (Company A), and that the first Ronald McDonald was Willard Scott. Did you know about Kroc's many failures, like the Hula Burger (a Friday-special pineapple sandwich for Cincinnati Catholics), Jane Dobbins Pies, or the San Diego Padres in the years Ray was alive?

Got a question? "Talk to Ray" in a phone-filled theater! Select McDonald's-related questions from a video menu, and Ray will resurrect before your eyes and answer them. When Kroc stated, "McDonald's is not a restaurant . . . It's a religion," he definitely cast himself as the Messiah.

McDonald's Corporation, 1 McDonald's Plaza, Oak Brook, IL 60521

(630) 623-3000

Hours: Monday–Friday 9A.M.–5P.M.

Cost: Free

www.mcdonalds.com/main.html

Directions: Just east of Oak Brook Shopping Center off Cermak Rd.

OAK PARK
Betty White was born in Oak Park on January 17, 1922.

Oak Park
Frank Lloyd Wright Studio and Museum

Frank Lloyd Wright, no matter what you might think of him, is arguably one of America's most influential architects. His first home in Oak Park is situated in the neighborhood where many of his early designs came to fruition. Wright built the place in 1889 at the age of 22 with a $5,000 loan from his employer, architect Louis Sullivan. Wright was fired four years later after Sullivan learned Wright was designing "bootleg" houses behind Sullivan's back.

Seeing Wright's work from the outside is always impressive, but visiting the interior is better: take the Home and Studio Tour. The guides on the Home and Studio Tour are quick to point out Wright's forward-thinking vision. The house was wired before Oak Park even provided electricity, baseboards for air conditioning vents were installed long before central air, and don't even ask them about that as-yet-unused teleportation room off the library. Jokes in the shadow of a genius are not welcome!

951 Chicago Ave., Oak Park, IL 60302

(708) 848-1976

Hours: Monday–Friday 11A.M., 1P.M., and 3P.M., Saturday–Sunday 11A.M.–3:30P.M.

Cost: Adults $8, Seniors (65+) $6, Kids (7–18) $6

www.wrightplus.org

Directions: At Forest Street, three blocks east of Harlem (Rte. 43).

"Broad Lawns and Narrow Minds"

Oak Park's most famous native son, Ernest Hemingway, once described this Chicago suburb as a place with "broad lawns and narrow minds." The folks here have since forgiven Ernie for the wisecrack, but you don't often hear them repeating it.

Ernest Hemingway was born in Oak Park on July 21, 1899. To announce the birth, his father Clarence stood on the front porch and blared his cornet. Ernest was also the apple of his mother's eye. His parents' dotage obviously affected his ego.

The family moved from Ernest's birthplace to a new home (161 N. Grove, not open to the public) when he was six years old, then soon to a third house (600 N. Kenilworth, not open to the public) where Ernest would live until he left Oak Park. Hemingway attended Holmes

Elementary School and Oak Park High School, where he wrote for the school paper, the *Trapeze*, played the cello, and managed the track team. There are many photos of Hemingway during this time, and in almost every one he looks pissed off.

The Hemingway Foundation has an excellent collection of Hemingway family artifacts, including Ernest's first book written at age two, zebra skin rugs, the manuscript of *Across the River and Into the Trees*, and the "Dear Ernest" letter he received from nurse Agnes von Kurowsky after returning to Oak Park to recuperate from war wounds.

Hemingway Birthplace, 339 N. Oak Park Ave. (formerly 439), Oak Park, IL 60302

(708) 848-2222

E-mail: ehfop@the Ramp.net

Hours: Thursday–Friday, Sunday 1–5P.M., Saturday 10A.M.–5P.M.

Cost: Adults $6, Kids $4.50 (includes museum)

Directions: One block north of the museum.

Hemingway Museum, 200 N. Oak Park Ave., Oak Park, IL 60302

(708) 848-2222

Hours: Thursday–Friday, Sunday, 1–5P.M., Saturday 10 A.M.–5P.M.

Cost: Adults $6, Kids $4.50 (includes birthplace)

www.hemingway.org

Directions: One block north of Lake St.

ORLAND PARK

Harrison Bailey was attacked by several gray aliens resembling frogs as he walked through the woods near Orland Park on September 24, 1951. Telepathically, they told Bailey they wanted him to be a spokesperson for them.

Orland Park claims to be "The Golf Capital of the World."

An Orland Park home was bulldozed in 1988 after investigators were unable to determine why flames continuously shot out of wall sockets. Some say it was the pig slaughterhouse once located on the land, or the two human graves unearthed during its construction.

Park Ridge
Museum of Anesthesiology

This museum won't leave you numb . . . but it could! Using the private collection of Dr. Paul Wood to start, the American Society of Anesthesiologists has amassed an impressive collection of literature, instruments, and numbing agents related to the history of anesthesiology. Displays are arranged by topic in somewhat chronological order.

The first anesthetics were administered as inhalants: ether, chloroform, and nitrous oxide. Though these gases' properties were known for years, it took some time before doctors suggested their use during surgery in the 1840s. There is debate as to who deserves the credit for the first use of ether—William Morton or Dr. Crawford Long—but whoever launched the idea, the practice caught on quick.

Although patients could be knocked out by inhalants, it wasn't until Dr. Richard and Ruth Gill brought rain forest curare to the medical establishment's attention that anesthesiology began resembling its modern form. Curare temporarily paralyzes a patient who has been knocked out, making it easier for a surgeon to operate.

You'll learn about curare, "laughing gas," and much more of the world of "doctors without patients" at the Wood Museum. Before you leave, you'll know the difference between an anesthetist and an anesthesiologist, how it was once common to administer ether rectally during childbirth, that opiates and cannabis were at one time tools of the trade, and why merger-mania is changing the face of anesthesiologists' equipment. Gas tanks, masks, monitors, acupuncture needles, Ecuadorian blow darts—they're all here!

Wood Library-Museum of Anesthesiology, 520 N. Northwest Highway,

Park Ridge, IL 60068-2573

(847) 825-5586

E-mail: wlm@ASAhq.org

Hours: Monday–Friday 9 A.M.–4:45 P.M.; call ahead to arrange a personal tour

Cost: Free

www.asahq.org/wlm

Directions: At the intersection of Northwest Highway and Greenwood Ave.

PARK RIDGE

Harrison Ford attended Maine Township High School in Park Ridge, graduating in 1960. He was in the Model Railroad Club.

River Grove
Hala Kahiki

"No food. No beer. Just tropical drinks." That's the way it was described on the phone. Could any place be that wonderful?

Well, Hala Kahiki comes close. South Seas decor. Hawaiian-dressed waitresses. And a tropical drink menu the size of a small phone book. Missionary's Downfall, Dr. Funk of Tahiti, Pineapple Boomerang, Skip & Run Naked, Suffering Bastard, Preacher's Panic Punch—where to start? Try them all, as long as you have a designated driver. The waitress will take the menu away between drinks, just in case you get a little sloppy, and you probably will. The drinks are cheap, and umbrellas are included.

The Hala Kahiki looks like it was built one room at a time. As you walk toward the rear, each turn through a doorway reveals another grouping of dimly lit tables. Finally, you reach a gift shop bursting with carved coconut monkey heads, fake grass skirts, shell lamps, and racks of Hawaiian shirts and mumus. If you're staggering, stay away from the tiki mugs on the shelves.

2834 River Rd., River Grove, IL 60171

(708) 456-3222

Hours: Monday–Tuesday 7p.m.–2a.m., Wednesday–Thursday 4p.m.–2a.m., Friday–Saturday 4p.m.–3a.m., Sunday 6p.m.–2a.m.

Cost: Drinks $2 and up

Directions: Just north of Grand Ave. on River Rd.

RIVER GROVE

John Belushi's parents, Agnes and John, are buried in River Grove's Elmwood Cemetery (2905 Thatcher). Their headstone implies that John might be laid to rest beside them, but he's actually planted on Martha's Vineyard in Massachusetts.

SKOKIE

Robert "Mr. Mike Brady" Reed is buried in Skokie's Memorial Park Cemetery (9900 Gross Point Rd.).

Ed Stockey points out some mighty fine whittlin'.

South Holland
Midwest Carver's Museum

The Midwest Carver's Museum is much more than a static display of regional artists; it's an active club of local carvers and whittlers (the South Suburban Chiselers), a gift shop, and a library covering all aspects of the pastime. It was founded in 1988 and shows no sign of slowing.

The museum is the first building you enter. It is guarded by two carved "busy beavers." On display are 1,000-plus pieces from midwestern woodworkers and a few samples from farther away. Many reflect common themes (cowboys, ducks, and more cowboys), but there is the occasional "odd duck," like the Odd Duck of a man's head on a mallard's body, or a whittling of Richard Nixon holding a bowling ball. In the basement is a library open to club members.

Adjoining the museum is a gift shop where you can buy knives, wood, and books. In back, small replicas of a saloon, a blacksmith shop, and homes are filled with small pieces from club members, none of which are for sale. A woodworking shop filled with jigsaws and hundreds of templates made by cofounder Ed Stockey stands to the south, and a converted home acts as a meeting place for people to try their hands at carving. Amateurs and pros gather around tables to swap advice and stories and pass along their craft.

16236 Vincinnes Ave., South Holland, IL 60473

(708) 331-6011

Hours: Monday–Saturday 10A.M.–4P.M.

Cost: Donations encouraged

Directions: Five blocks east of Halsted and one block south of 162nd (Rte. 6).

Willowbrook
Flower Pot and Arap

Flower Pot was a skunk. A very special skunk. So special, in fact, that when he died his owner buried him in a formal cemetery and topped the grave with a life-sized sculpture of the stinker.

There have been plenty of deceased animals like Flower Pot lovingly laid to rest in Hinsdale Animal Cemetery since it opened in 1926. While most are dogs and cats, there are the occasional birds, turtles, horses, and a deer named Bambi. The most impressive monument is for a dog named Arap, whose headstone reads, "He Gave Up His Life That a Human Might Live. Greater Love Hath No Man." Walking through the well-kept cemetery, it is hard not to be touched by the sentiments of these animals' owners, especially as you see etched tombstones with photos of beagles in Santa hats and Persian cats on big, fluffy pillows.

Hinsdale Animal Cemetery, 6400 S. Bentley Ave., Willowbrook, IL 60514

(630) 323-5120

E-mail: hinsancem@aol.com

Hours: Monday–Friday 9A.M.–5P.M., Saturday–Sunday 8A.M.–3P.M.

Cost: Free; burials extra

www.petcemetery.org

Directions: One block south of 63rd, three blocks west of Clarendon Hills Rd.

Needed: The World's Largest Orange.

Wilmette
Bahá'í House of Worship

Looking like a gigantic, nine-sided orange juice squeezer on the shores of Lake Michigan, the Bahá'í House of Worship is the only such structure in North America. It was designed by Louis Bourgeois and is constructed of cement panels made with a concrete/quartz mixture, which becomes a sparkling beacon at night. The white panels were cast in Washington, D.C.

and shipped to Wilmette by rail where they took more than 40 years to assemble. The Chicago area's largest jigsaw puzzle was dedicated on May 2, 1953, and is open to the general public.

100 Linden Ave., Wilmette, IL 60091

(847) 853-2300

Hours: May–September, daily 10A.M.–10P.M.; October–April, daily 10A.M.–5P.M.

Cost: Free

Directions: Along the lake, off Sheridan Rd.

Worth
Rose Mary and Mayor Daley

Mary Alice Quinn, "The Little Flower," was a pious 14-year-old who had dedicated herself to St. Therese of Lisieux, but that didn't prevent the teenager's death in 1935. Some who knew her believed she had been given the gift of healing, and that it continued even after her untimely death. Visitors to her grave reported the smell of roses, even in the dead of winter, then received miraculous cures. Mary Alice Quinn was nicknamed Rose Mary.

Word got around and soon hundreds were praying at her grave. Reportedly, if Rose Mary answered your prayers, you would smell roses on the ninth day after your request. Anxious to connect with her, some pilgrims would take soil from her grave, and groundskeepers needed to replace the soil lest she be unearthed. Fewer people visit Rose Mary's grave today, but you're still likely to see somebody there if you visit.

If you go to Holy Sepulchre Cemetery on the morning of a Chicago election, you're likely to find somebody famous at a grave other than Rose Mary's: Richard M. Daley at the plot of his father, Richard J. Daley. The young Daley has made it a tradition of visiting the man who defined

---

WILMETTE

Bill Murray was born in Wilmette on September 21, 1950. He graduated from Loyola Academy in 1968.

WORTH

Muddy Waters, born McKinley Morganfield, is buried in Restvale Cemetery (117th & Laramie), the cemetery of choice for Chicago Blues legends.

Machine Politics on the most important day of the year, at least for deceased Cook County residents; this is the one day where their votes count! No doubt Daley is there to ask for his father's support.

Holy Sepulchre Cemetery, 6001 111th St.. Worth, IL 60482

(708) 422-3020

Hours: September–April, daily 8:30A.M.–5P.M.; May–August, daily 8:30A.M.–7P.M.

Cost: Free

Directions: Bound between 111th and 115th Sts., and Central and Ridgeland Aves. Daley is to the immediate left as you enter. Quinn is buried in Section 7, to the right, just behind the large red "Capone" monument.

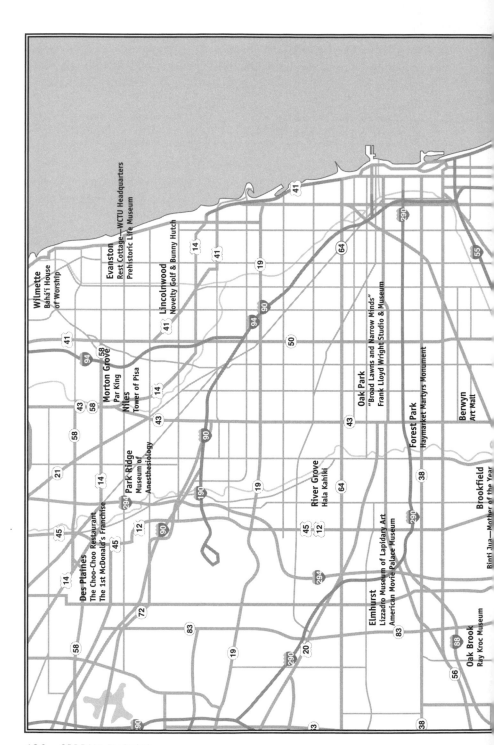

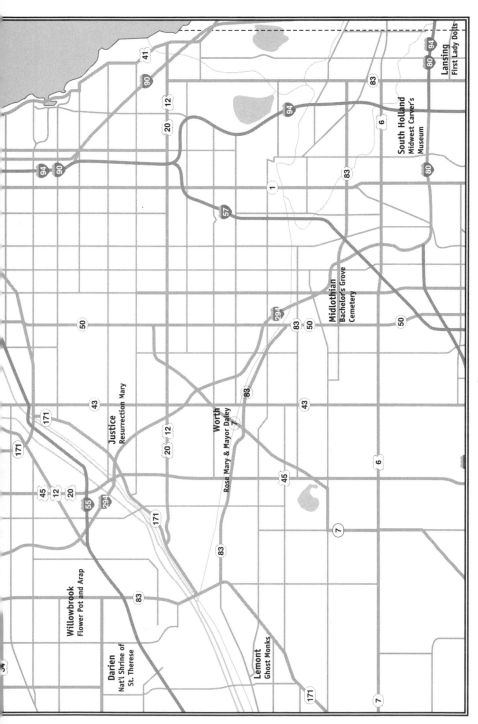

NORTHERN ILLINOIS

3

*W*ere it not for the work of Nathaniel Pope, this might have been a very short book. When drafting the original borders for Illinois, Congress marked its northern boundary at the southern tip of Lake Michigan, 61 miles south of where it is today. But Pope, a territorial senator from the region, offered a proposal to move the boundary farther north, from 41°37' to 42°30', in order to give the future state a port on the lake. The proposal passed, and when Illinois became a state in 1818, Fort Dearborn, the future Chicago, was on the Illinois side.

Think about it. If Congress had kept its original boundaries, folks in Northern Illinois might be wearing Cheese Hats! And would the Badger State have spawned such wonder-filled regional attractions as Donley's Wild West Town, Santa's Village, or Lambs Farm, at least outside the Dells tourist vortex? Maybe. Maybe not. But this I know for sure: because these places are in Illinois, their gift shops aren't crammed with cow-abilia and coolers full of cheese. That's something.

109

Aledo
A Night Spent in Jail

If you've got to spend the weekend in jail as part of some plea bargain, do it in Aledo. The food's fantastic, they've got a sauna and a jacuzzi, and they hand you the keys to come and go as you please. Sound like they're coddling criminals? Did I mention that this is a bed and breakfast?

Housed in the 1909 Mercer County Jail, The Great Escape lacks the rifle-toting guards and shower fights of most correctional facilities. Instead, they've got comfy rooms, free popcorn and soda, and friendly "jailers." If all prisons were this nice, people would be killing one another to get in.

Downstairs is the Slammer Restaurant, offering entrees such as a Fishy Story, an Executioner's Order, or a Final Request. Each booth is its own cell, circa 1909, and the waiters and waitresses wear striped uniforms. If you're rowdy, there's a padded cell, and if the kids act up, you can always threaten them with the electric chair. It's on the second floor.

The Great Escape B&B/Slammer Restaurant, 309 S. College Ave., Aledo, IL 61231

(309) 582-5359

Hours: Year round; call for reservations

Cost: Single $55, Double $65

www.bbonline.com/il/ilbba/members/greatescape.html

Directions: Just southwest of the town square.

Aurora
African American Heritage Cultural Center

Tucked away on a side street on the east side of Aurora, in an area where zoning laws don't seem to be a problem, is a remarkable folk art environment built by Dr. Charles Smith. He named the place the African American Heritage Cultural Center, but it's more of a lean-to art studio surrounded by hundreds of sculptural pieces. Smith describes it as a "complete historical collage of the African American Experience," and he's probably right. His 400+ statues are arranged in roughly chronological order starting on the North Avenue side of the lot and sweeping around to the front of his studio.

If you're looking for a specific historic figure or event relating to African American history, he'll help you find it. While the outside sculptures are strictly statues, the works he has in his studio are often functional household items, like human-form lamps or a series of Hattie McDaniel hot plate holders. Plug them in—they work!

When you visit the site, be sure to allot some time to talk to Dr. Smith. No visit would be complete without spending a few minutes as one of his (as he calls you) "sequestered jurors." This former U.S. Marine and Vietnam veteran will gladly share his thoughts on why places like the DuSable Museum don't hold a candle to his creation, how Oprah Winfrey has become accepted by such a wide audience, and the reason he doesn't have as many visitors as he deserves. You may not agree with any of his ideas, but at least you'll know where he stands.

126 S. Kendall, PO Box 334, Aurora, IL 60505

(630) 375-0657

Hours: Call ahead for an appointment; statues always visible from the road

Cost: Free

Directions: I-88 to Farnsworth Ave., south to North Ave., east to Kendall.

Barrington
JFK Health World

If you want your child to pick up a few pointers on healthy living, or to learn a few things for yourself, JFK Health World is the place. Hundreds of hands-on exhibits on three levels allow kids to crawl through the human heart; perform surgery; fill a giant cavity; sandwich themselves between tumbling mats of bread, bologna, and cheese; play an engineer on a Metra train trying to dodge Yuppie commuters; ride in an ambulance as an Emergency Medical Technician or as a crash victim; and more.

The best interactive display is a wall of cigarette packs where the cost of basketball shoes, video game cartridges, and in-line skates are translated for the nicotine addict. Let's see, if you're a three-pack-a-day smoker, it would only take 12 days for you to inhale the cost of a pair of sneakers!

1301 S. Grove Ave., Barrington, IL 60010

(847) 842-9100

Hours: Monday–Thursday 10A.M.–3P.M., Friday 10A.M.–8P.M., Saturday–Sunday 10A.M.–3P.M.

Cost: Adults $5, Kids $5

www.jfkhealthworld.com

Directions: Two blocks east of Barrington Rd., one block north of Dundee Rd. (Rte. 68).

ALEDO

Every June the town of Aledo has a Rhubarb Festival.

Batavia
Mary Todd Lincoln in the Cuckoo's Nest

After her husband's assassination, Mary Todd Lincoln went off the deep end. She told people that gas lamps were sent from the Devil, that unknown persons were pulling wires from her eyes and bones from her left cheek, and that an Indian spirit lived in her head, causing her constant headaches. He even, on one occasion, removed and replaced her scalp, according to Mary.

In 1875 her son Robert had her committed to a sanitarium after an embarrassing public trial pitting son against mother. Mary ended up in the Bellevue Place Rest Home, an unconventional "rest home" by any standards. According to *The Insanity Files* (Neely & McMurtry, 1986), "patients received quinine, morphia, marijuana, cod-liver oil, beer or ale . . . [T]he staff seems only to have kept order while allowing the patients to play croquet, go for walks around the grounds, take carriage rides, or play the piano." If that's institutionalization, sign me up!

Mary didn't stay long and was soon released on an "experiment." During that time, those around her learned that she was planning to kill her son Robert, even carrying a pistol in her pocket. It never happened, but she did send him a long series of letters demanding back the gifts she had previously lavished on Robert, renamed "the monster of mankind," and his wife. Mary went to live with her sister in Springfield and almost drove her nuts, living in the dark until her death on July 15, 1882.

The building where Lincoln was held, stoned and playing croquet, is now a private condominium complex. She did not stay in the main "Ell" of the building, but in the residence adjacent to the main structure.

Private Residences, 333 S. Jefferson St., Batavia, IL 60510

Mary Todd Lincoln Display, Batavia Depot Museum, 155 Houston, Batavia, IL 60510

(708) 879-5235

Hours: April–November, Monday, Wednesday, Friday–Sunday 2–4 P.M.

Cost: Free

members.aol.com/RVSNorton/Lincoln22.html

Directions: One block north of Wilson St., one block east of Batavia Ave. (Rte. 31).

BATAVIA

Batavia is nicknamed "The Windmill City" because of the large number of farming windmills manufactured here.

Belvidere
Big Thunder Park

Chief Big Thunder of the Potawatomie tribe wanted to be buried in such a way that he would be able to command future generations in battle, which is to say, he did not want to be buried at all. After dying in the 1830s he was wrapped in a blanket and placed in a chair atop the tallest hill around. A stash of earthly belongings and tobacco were laid out around him. Big Thunder's body was guarded only by a six-foot-tall stockade fence through which a hole had been cut for him to peer out at the Squaw Prairie. This land was where he predicted the future battle would take place.

The elements and vultures had their way, but it was the tourists that did him in. Stagecoach passengers who stopped in Belvidere at Doty's Tavern were encouraged to stretch their legs by walking up the hill to view Big Thunder's body and leave a tobacco offering. The chief's skull soon disappeared (some think it ended up in the hands of an East Coast phrenologist), and the rest of the bones were up for grabs.

Local residents then faced a dilemma: see their tourist trap disappear or come up with a plan. Kids began tossing animal bones into the stockade so visitors never went away empty-handed. Many travelers went home with a soup bone from a local slaughterhouse, and many local kids collected free tobacco from the city suckers.

The scheme didn't work forever. The first Boone County Courthouse was built on the same hill, and a flagpole was erected on the spot where Big Thunder's chair sat. The DAR attached a plaque to a boulder by the flagpole, and that's all you'll see today.

601 N. Main St., Belvidere, IL 61008

Hours: Always visible

Cost: Free

Directions: On the front lawn of the Old Boone County Courthouse, two blocks east of State St. (Rte. 20 Business).

BOLINGBROOK

Bolingbrook resident Beatrice Oczki burst into flames while watching TV on November 24, 1979. The beer in her hand exploded, two of her dogs asphyxiated, and a VCR tape melted. Oczki was reduced from 195 to 40 pounds in just seconds.

Wile E. Coyote would be right at home.

Big Rock
Mount Barry

Jutting up from the banks of Welch Creek is a teetering tower of red rock. A natural formation? Hardly. It looks more like a movie set from a Road Runner cartoon. Saguaro cacti made of rebar cling to the mountain, as do several plastic barrel cacti and a small concrete deer.

Welcome to Mount Barry, also known as Arizona Mountain, the creation of John Van Barriger. This Big Rock resident has always had an affection for the Southwest and decided to make his own Monument Valley in the heart of corn country. Building permits be damned, Mount Barry went up, made mostly of concrete slabs and other salvaged construction material.

Kane County officials were not happy about the new big rock in Big Rock. They've tried to fine Van Barriger for toxins supposedly leaching into the creek, but they were hard pressed to prove concrete is poisonous. For the time being, Mount Barry stands tall, but you'd better get a quick look before the county kill-joys fire up a bulldozer.

Route 30, Big Rock, IL 60511

Private phone

Hours: Always visible

Cost: Free

Directions: South on Rte. 30 where it intersects with Dauberman Rd., across the railroad tracks.

Bull Valley
Stickney Mansion

What blood is to Dracula, square corners are to the Devil. Satan *loves* to hide in square corners . . . at least that's what George and Sylvia Stickney believed. When their Bull Valley mansion was constructed in 1849, masons were under strict orders not to build it with any 90-degree corners. From the outside, it appears that they did a good job rounding off the points, but apparently they overlooked the meeting of two interior walls.

Sylvia and George were Spiritualists and through seances confirmed their worst fear: the Devil was going to pay them a visit. One day, George was found huddled in the only square corner of the house, dead from no apparent cause. Sylvia packed up and never returned.

Subsequent owners reported hearing George's ghost, including a band of "devil worshippers" in the 1960s. Well, the locals thought they were devil worshippers, but they were actually a hippie commune. The building fell into disrepair in the 1970s until it was put into service as the Bull Valley Village Hall. You're welcome to stop by during business hours, but the upper floor is off limits. Could it be the Village knows something you don't? Stay out of the corners . . .

1904 Cherry Valley Rd., Bull Valley, IL 60098

(815) 459-4833

Hours: Always visible on outside; inside Monday–Friday 10A.M.–5P.M.

Cost: Free

Directions: Just north of Crystal Springs Rd.

DeKalb
The Egyptian Theater

Built in 1928 and opened in 1929, the Egyptian Theater puts the modern moviegoing experience to shame. Architect Elmer Baron used features from the tomb of Ramses II to make the Egyptian a special place, such as a scarab skylight, linen curtains, and two seated Ramses II statues flanking the stage. A ceiling peppered with twinkling stars and a cloud generator gave visitors the illusion they were seated in a desert oasis, as did the murals depicting the Pyramids of Giza, the Sphinx, and the tableaus of Abu Simbal.

But the Egyptian fell on hard times. It was to be torn down in 1976, but it was purchased by a group of volunteers calling themselves P.E.T.: Preserve the Egyptian Theater. It was 1983 before the building was renovated. P.E.T. managed to keep 80 percent of the original building intact, including the antique carbon-arc projector. The murals were restored with a few minor revisions. Look for the tablets showing the restorers' names at the front left, or the cat on the rock at the front right. A stray cat became the constant companion of restoration crews, so it was immortalized.

The 1,475-seat Egyptian does not just show movies on weekends. It also has about 40 to 50 live performances a year. Call ahead for a schedule.

135 N. Second St., PO Box 385, DeKalb, IL 60115

(815) 758-1215

Hours: Call ahead for a performance schedule; closed January, July, and August

Cost: Adults $4.50, Kids $3; tours free

Directions: One block north of Lincoln Highway (Rte. 38), two blocks west of Rte. 23.

Corn? Corn? What's corn?

Dixon
Ronald Reagan's Boyhood Home

Ronald Reagan's family moved to Dixon when "Dutch" was just nine years old. It was here, in "The Petunia Capital of the World," that Ronnie learned to swim at the YMCA, where he ran around with his brother Neil, or "Moon" as the other kids knew him, and where he was Art Director for the 1928 school yearbook.

The Reagan family lived in this home from 1920 to 1923. None of the furnishings here are original; they were chosen from a pre-1920 Sears catalog by the former President according to what he remembered, which wasn't much. (Actually, his brother Moon later admitted that neither he nor Ron remembered too much about this place, moving around as much as their family did.) In front of the home stands a statue of Reagan as President, staring into his upturned palm. A plaque reads, "Illinois is famous for its production of agricultural products, so it seems appropriate for him to be admiring the kernels of corn in his hand."

Other Dixon homes in which his family lived (338 W. Everett Ave., 226 Lincolnway, and 107–108 Monroe Ave.) are not open to the public.

816 S. Hennepin Ave., Dixon, IL 61021

(815) 288-3404

Hours: April–November, Monday–Saturday 10A.M.–4P.M., Sunday 1–4P.M.; December–March, Saturday 10A.M.–4P.M., Sunday 1–4P.M.

Cost: Free

www.dixonil.com/attractions.htm

Directions: Just west of Galena Ave., south of downtown.

East Dundee
Santa's Village

Where does St. Nick spend the off season? East Dundee, of course! He might make house calls on Christmas Day, but for the rest of the year, little boys and girls must come to Illinois if they want to speak to him.

Santa's Village is divided into three "worlds": Old McDonald's Farm, Coney Island, and Santa's World. Outside of Santa's Village, these "worlds" would be called a petting zoo, an amusement park, and a kiddie land. Some rides have been given winter-ish names, like The Snowball and The Himalaya, or they've dressed them up with candy canes, elves, snowmen, and toadstools. Apparently, the North Pole is covered in brightly colored mushrooms.

Don't think this place is just for the little tykes. They've also got a looping roller coaster, a shooting gallery, and best of all, beer!

Rtes. 25 and 72, East Dundee, IL 60118

(847) 426-6751

E-mail: FunForKids@aol.com

Hours: June–August, daily 10A.M.–6P.M. (8P.M. weekends); May, September, Saturday–Sunday 10A.M.–6P.M.

Cost: Adults $15.95, Kids $15.95, Group discounts available

www.santasvillageil.com

Directions: At the intersection of Rte. 72 and Rte. 25.

FOX LAKE

Seven-foot-tall skeletons have reportedly been unearthed on Point Comfort Hill in Fox Lake.

Galena
The Green Drapes

Contrary to what was depicted in *Gone with the Wind*, Miss Scarlett did not make Tara's drapes into a dress. Need proof? They're hanging right here in the Belvedere Mansion! And that's not all. This place has also got oil paintings from Tara and Victorian trinkets picked up at Liberace's estate sale. This Galena abode is the restored Italianate mansion of a former ambassador to Belgium, J. Russell Jones, and is one of the fanciest homes in "The Town That Time Forgot."

Belvedere Mansion, 1008 Park Ave., Galena, IL 61036

(815) 777-0747

Hours: June–October, Sunday–Friday 11A.M.–4P.M., Saturday 11A.M.–5P.M.

Cost: Adults $5, Kids $2.50

Directions: Off Rte. 20 before you reach the bridge, heading west.

Kewanee
Woodland Palace

Fred Francis was a lot of things—an engineer, a vegetarian, a believer in reincarnation, a Physical Culturalist, an agnostic, a nudist—but most locals just thought he was a nut. They weren't entirely wrong, but Francis was a brilliant nut.

A mechanical genius, he patented a watch-making tool for the Elgin Watch Company during the 1880s and was able to retire in his early thirties, living only on his royalties. But his retirement was far from restful. Francis set out in 1890 to build Woodland Palace for himself and his new bride, Jeanie Crowfoot.

Though small and not wired for electricity, Woodland Palace was air conditioned in the summer, warmed through radiant heat in the winter, and had hundreds of modern mechanical conveniences. Storm windows and screens rolled in and out of use depending on the season, and a windmill pumped running water from a filtered cistern. It also powered a workshop in his basement.

His land was surrounded by a large hedge because Francis was a Physical Culturalist and practicing nudist. He seldom wore shoes, wanting to keep his feet in contact with the soil, and when he was at home, he was usually nude. Jeanie did not participate in her husband's activities, but if she objected, she did not show it.

Francis was left heartbroken after Jeanie died of tuberculosis. He continued to live in the home they shared, but when a hernia became too painful to bear, he killed himself. His will asked that he be cremated in a coffinlike cage on the property, but Illinois prevented this final wish.

Francis Park, Route 34, Kewanee, IL 61443

(309) 852-0511

Hours: Late April–Late October, Monday–Friday 1–5p.m., Saturday–Sunday 10a.m.–5p.m.

Cost: Adults $1, Kids 50¢

www.kewanee-il.com/cocmenu.htm

Directions: Rte. 34 north to 2800E, north to 900N, east to Woodland Park.

Do what he says and nobody gets hurt.

Libertyville
Lambs Farm Giant

Normally, fiberglass giants aren't frightening. You can see them on our nation's highways, dutifully holding tires and bags of groceries, but the Lambs Farm Giant is an exception—he's swinging an ax! And from the look on the face of the cow beside him, you know he plans to use it.

The Giant guards the miniature golf course and petting zoo at Lambs Farm, a working facility for persons with mental disabilities in Chicago's north suburbs. Residents assist in the day-to-day operations of the bakery, country store, thrift shop, and other enterprises, receiving vocational education in a community setting.

Perhaps the big guy with the ax is here to protect the admirable work of this institution. Keep thinking that . . . try not to tick him off.

Lambs Farm, PO Box 520, Libertyville, IL 60048

(847) 362-4636

Hours: Daily 9A.M.–6P.M.

Cost: Free; golf $3.00 per person per game

www.lambsfarm.com

Directions: At the intersection of Rte. 176 and I-94.

Head ornament.

Mt. Carroll
Raven's Grin Inn

To call Raven's Grin Inn a haunted house is to call Disneyland a carnival. It's so much more. Raven's Grin Inn is a childhood clubhouse gone haywire, an indoor junkyard fun house, a performance art piece that could have been built by the Marx Brothers, but it's actually the 14-year-old brainchild of Jim Warfield.

Warfield promises "No chainsaws, No Jason, No Freddy!" but that doesn't mean you won't be frightened or entertained. Without revealing too much, it's safe to say you'll spend a full hour crawling through passageways, bumping down slides, jumping at sight gags, meeting Mr. Tuxedo (Warfield's cat), and listening to creepy monologues worthy of a dead Henny Youngman.

The visit will take you at least an hour, more if you get lost, and you probably will, no thanks to your tour guide. When offered the "optional ride" midway through your visit, take it, and hold on. There are multiple paths through the 1870s structure, so no two visits will ever be the same.

Warfield hopes one day to make part of the Raven's Grin into a bed and breakfast where guests play a role in taunting the visitors. He already offers the Raven's Grin to Hide-and-Seek parties, so if you have a large group, call ahead.

411 N. Carroll St., Mt. Carroll, IL 61053

(815) 244-GRIN

Hours: Friday–Saturday 2–5 p.m., 7–11 p.m., Sunday–Thursday 7–11 p.m.; call ahead for reservations

Cost: Adults $8

Directions: Behind the True Value, just north of the business district.

Norway
A Crashed Plane

You might be tempted to call 911 when you spot a plane crashed nose down on a country road near Norway, but you'd be reporting a tragedy that happened a decade ago, and it had nothing to do with airplanes. A sign in front of the wreck reads, "Dedicated to farmers and all ag-related business folks that have lived thru the agricultural crash of the 1980s." It was erected by Melvin and Phyllis Eastwold of the Norwegian Implement Company.

While you could stare at the empty shell and contemplate the farm crisis, it would be a shame to pass up a great photo opportunity. Lie on the ground as if thrown from the fuselage on impact and you'll always be able to trump your friends with vacation horror stories.

Route 71, Norway, IL 60551

Hours: Always visible

Cost: Free

Directions: South of town on Rte. 71.

LIBERTYVILLE

Marlon Brando lived in Libertyville from 1936 to 1943. He worked for some time as an usher at the local theater, but after being fired he crammed rotten broccoli and Limburger cheese into the air conditioning system.

Oregon
Big Chief Black Hawk

Overlooking the Rock River Valley is a stoic Native American figure, 48 feet from head to toe. It is the Largest Reinforced Concrete Statue in the World, a massive monument weighing 268 tons and sitting on a foundation that goes 30 feet into the ground. It is commonly referred to as Big Chief Black Hawk, but the name is incorrect. While it could be many Native Americans, it looks nothing like Chief Black Hawk; he had a mohawk.

The statue is the work of Lorado Taft, leader of the Eagle's Nest Artist Colony during the 1920s. This group of Chicago "bohemians" set up shop near Oregon each summer to escape the heat and frighten the locals. Taft's previous artist colony had been run out of Indiana, and the folks of Oregon were only slightly more receptive. It could have been the constant fun everyone seemed to be having, or the plaster sculptures they made one day and smashed the next, but most likely it was the themed evenings. One night the entire colony dressed in Egyptian garb, paraded around the bluffs, and presented two "slaves" to a visiting Egyptologist.

Lowden State Park, PO Box 403, 1411 N. River Rd., Oregon, IL 61061

(815) 732-6828

Hours: Daily sunrise–sunset

Cost: Free

dnr.state.il.us/lands/landmgt/parks/lowdensp.htm

Directions: Route 64 east from Oregon, turn north on River Rd., follow the signs in the park.

Ottawa
Effigy Tumuli

Many early American cultures built effigy mounds, earthen sculptures formed in the shapes of animals to honor great spirits (or to signal UFOs if you believe *Chariots of the Gods*). But there is another possibility for why some mounds exist: to cover up a mess.

That was the plan behind Effigy Tumuli, designed by Michael Heizer. As part of a land reclamation project on the Rock River, these five modern earthen mounds were piled in the shape of a snake, a catfish, a water strider, a frog, and a turtle. Because they're a mile and a half long and mostly flat, they can only be truly appreciated from the air, though you're welcome to hike all over them.

Buffalo Rock State Park, PO Box 2034, Ottawa, IL 61350

(815) 433-2220

Hours: Sunrise–Sunset

Cost: Free

slaggarden.cfa.cmu.edu/weblinks/frost/FrostTop.html

Directions: Two miles west of town on Dee Bennett Rd., along the Rock River.

Ottawa Scouting Museum

W. D. Boyce was a world traveler, yet somehow he got lost on a foggy London evening in July 1909. A young boy emerged from the mist and helped him find where he was going. When Boyce offered the lad a tip, the boy refused, saying it was part of his duties as a Boy Scout to "Do a good turn every day." Boyce knew he wouldn't be the only guy who would ever get lost in the fog, so he met with British Scout founder Colonel Baden-Powell. In 1910, Boyce established an American chapter to assist others with a poor sense of direction.

Boyce was able to fund the early Scouts using money he made through the un-scoutsmanlike enterprise of publishing tabloid newspapers in Chicago. He had enough left over to purchase an estate near Ottawa. When he died in 1929, Boyce was buried in the Ottawa Avenue Cemetery, and a Scouting Monument was placed over his grave in 1941.

Because of Ottawa's Boyce connection, it is the natural place for a Scouting Museum. The newly opened collection has an impressive array of memorabilia associated with the Boy Scouts of America, the Lone Scouts, the Girl Scouts, the Brownies, the Camp Fire Girls, and others.

1100 Canal St., PO Box 2241, Ottawa, IL 61350

(815) 431-9353

Hours: Thursday–Monday 10A.M.–4P.M.

Cost: Adults $3, Kids $2

homepage.dave-world.net/~wdboyce/council/locations/ottawa_scout_museum.htm

Directions: Four blocks west of Columbus (Rte. 23) along Washington.

TROY GROVE

James Butler "Wild Bill" Hickok was born in Troy Grove on May 27, 1837. A monument to Wild Bill now stands in the town's park.

Union
Wild Wild Midwest

If you want to see a shoot-out but can't make it to Chicago, you can always visit Donley's Wild West Town. The killings look realistic, and you don't run the risk of getting caught in the cross fire—it's just acting! And that's not all, partner. You can pan for gold, knock back a few tall ones at the saloon, ride a pony, or get tossed in jail for a minor infraction. They've got roping demonstrations, a prairie dog town, a blacksmith, and a museum filled with guns, old phonographs, Beanie Babies, and other Old West artifacts.

Wild West Town used to have a wider and weirder collection of memorabilia on display, but more sensitive concerns have taken over. No longer will you see the Cook County gallows, bought from the city after it gave up hope of finding escaped murderer "Terrible" Tommy O'Connor. (Because he was explicitly sentenced to be hanged, they kept it until 1977, just in case.) The museum also had Hitler's 1908 red-leather photo album from World War I and a few of Adolf's *Mein Kampfs*, but they've been mothballed. But you will see six criminals' death masks from Pop Palmer's Freak Circus, including Bob Dalton and Cherokee Bill, as well as an autographed Tiny Tim album.

Donley's Wild West Town, 8512 S. Union Rd., Union, IL 60180

(815) 923-9000

E-mail: info@wildwesttown.com

Hours: April–May, September–October, Saturday–Sunday 10A.M.–6P.M.; June–August, daily 10A.M.–6P.M.; shoot-outs Noon, 2P.M., and 4:30P.M.

Cost: Adults(13+) $8, Kids(4–12) $8

www.wildwesttown.com

Directions: On Rte. 20, four miles north of I-90.

UTICA
Utica claims to be "The Burgoo Capital of the World." Burgoo is a soup made from vegetables and slow, free-roaming critters.

WAUCONDA
Marshall Applewhite and an early band of **Heaven's Gate** UFO followers camped at the Chain O' Lakes State Park near Spring Grove in 1975.

Pharaoh's Phortress.

Wadsworth
Gold Pyramid House

When James Onan broke ground for his ultimate dream house, a 1/100 replica of the Great Pyramid, the bulldozer struck a huge rock. Water spewed forth from the crack, flooding the site. Onan brought a chunk of the stone to a mineral assayist and learned that it contained gold, an element not found naturally in Illinois. Onan saw this as an omen to continue building.

The new natural spring feeds a moat around his six-story home, guarded by a large metal gate and a 40-foot, 200-ton Ramses II statue made by Walt Disney Studios. The pyramid is the World's Largest 24-karat-Gold-Plated Structure and is surrounded by the moat filled with, at times, jellyfish and live sharks. If you didn't know better, you'd think Onan was a James Bond villain.

Inside the structure is a recreation of King Tut's Tomb along with his gold-plated chariot. You can take a tour, but you have to arrange it in advance.

37921 Dilley's Rd., Wadsworth, IL 60083

(847) 662-6666, (847) 244-7777 for group tours

Hours: By appointment only

Cost: Adults $20

www.goldpyramid.com

Directions: 2.5 miles north of Great America (Rte. 132), adjacent to I-94.

Wauconda
Curt Teich Post Card Archives

The Lake County Museum is a better than average local historical museum, but the Curt Teich Post Card Archives make it exceptional. The Archives house a 1.5-million piece postcard collection, including every piece produced by the Curt Teich Company between 1898 and 1975. Teich's postcard salesmen were outfitted with cameras to take photos across the nation to make into cards. The company would later return to sell these cards to the communities in which they were taken, and as a result, they record a broad snapshot of America during the last century.

You can't actually use the archives unless you're a scholar or have a definable purpose, but you can see a rotating exhibit in the museum. If you have a project, discuss it with the staff and perhaps they can assist you.

Lake County Museum, Lake County Forest Preserve, 27277 Forest Preserve Dr., Wauconda, IL 60084

(847) 526-7878

Hours: Monday–Saturday 11A.M.–4:30P.M., Sunday 1–4:30P.M.

Cost: Adults $2.50, Kids(4–17) $1, Tuesdays free

www.co.lake.il.us/forest/ctpa.htm

Directions: Rte. 176W and Fairfield Rd.

Wheaton
Billy Graham Center Museum

Long called "The Button of the Bible Belt," Wheaton is home to 24 different religious organizations, the most prominent being Wheaton College, alma mater of Billy Graham. The evangelist graduated with a degree in anthropology in 1943. It is here that he met his wife, Ruth Bell, and where they set up their first and only pastorate: a Baptist church in Western Springs.

Though it is called the Billy Graham Center Museum, it actually traces the history of evangelism. The exhibits tend to skip over much of the burn-in-Hell stuff and spend more time talking about the Underground Railroad and the center's wonderful work with the underprivileged through the Salvation Army and the YMCA. In other words, this is a one-sided presentation.

One uncensored part of the museum, however, is its collection of Billy-abilia. They've got his traveling pulpit, a B+ paper he once wrote about Christopher Columbus, a plaque commemorating his star's placement on the Hollywood Walk of Fame, and photos of him with all the U.S. Presidents since Truman, as well as Johnny Cash, Sammy Davis, Jr., and Muhammed Ali.

Billy Graham Center Museum, Wheaton College, 500 E. College Ave.,
Wheaton, IL 60187-5593

(630) 752-5909

Hours: Monday–Saturday 9:30A.M.–5:30P.M., Sunday 1–5P.M.

Cost: Donations encouraged

www.wheaton.edu/bgc/bgcgeninfo.html

Directions: On campus off Main St., three blocks west of President St.

WAUKEGAN

Benjamin Kubelsky, better known as **Jack Benny**, was born in Waukegan (518 Clayton) on Valentine's Day, 1894.

WHEATON

John Belushi attended Wheaton Central High School, graduating in 1967. He was the Homecoming King.

Contemplating
the rocket.

Wilmington
The Gemini Giant
Never let it be said that the folks of Wilmington are behind the times. After a local business purchased a 30-foot, 500-pound lumberman at auction in 1965, they retrofitted the guy for a trip to the moon . . . and beyond! The Gemini Giant has stood guard over a local burger joint ever since.

The Gemini Giant wears a glimmering green jumpsuit straight out of *Lost in Space*, and a trashcan-like helmet. He stares out through the faceplate at a small rocket he holds in his hands. This is the third rocket the Giant has owned; two rockets have been stolen over the years, and the one he grips today was ripped off in 1992. It was later found in a cornfield and returned, much to NASA's relief.

Launching Pad Cafe, Route 53, Wilmington, IL 60481

(815) 476-6535

Hours: Always visible

Cafe Hours: Monday–Friday 9A.M.–10P.M., Saturday–Sunday 9A.M.–10:30P.M.

Cost: Free

Directions: On Old Route 66 at the east end of town.

Woodstock
Elvira in Seat DD 113

If you ever attend a performance at the Woodstock Opera House, don't sit in seat DD 113. That's Elvira's seat.

Who's Elvira? The legend goes that she was a young woman who hung herself in the bell tower, or tossed herself from the roof, after being jilted by an actor in 1903. (Other stories say she was a bitter actress passed over for a choice role.) Since her untimely death she has acted as the theater's resident critic, letting her sentiments be known on the quality of the Opera House's productions.

Elvira usually shows up during rehearsals, getting up and sitting down many times in seat DD 113, causing the springs to squeak uncontrollably. The more the seat squeaks, the worse the show is. Both Orsen Welles and Paul Newman claimed to have felt her presence at the theater.

Woodstock Opera House, 121 Van Buren St., Woodstock, IL 60098

(815) 338-5300

Hours: Box office daily 9A.M.–5P.M.; they will let you go inside if the lights are on

Cost: Depends on the show; free without show

Directions: On the square.

ZION

Gary Coleman was born in Zion on February 8, 1968.

Tan shoes? Shorts?
A globe? A movie?
Four-time Zion felon!

Zion
Flat Earth Town

Zion was founded in 1901 by John Alexander Dowie, head of a movement he called the Christian Catholic Church. At its peak the church had
6,000 followers in the so-called City of God: Zion City. The town was
essentially a theocracy with laws based upon the Old Testament and its
streets given prophetic names like Gabriel, Ezekiel, and Jethro. And
although Dowie was a stern patriarch, he was nothing compared to his
deputy, Wilbur Glenn Voliva.

Voliva took control around 1905. He ruled the town with an iron fist, outlawing alcohol, tobacco, circuses, opium, humming, movies, oysters, opera, pork, short pants, doctors, silk stockings, cosmetics, whistling on Sundays, tan-colored or high-heeled shoes, and most especially globes. Why globes? Voliva was sure of one thing: the Earth was flat. He scorned the "so-called fundamentalists [who] strain out the gnat of evolution and swallow the camel of modern astronomy."

According to Voliva, we live on a pancake with the North Pole at the center and the South Pole wrapping the edges. A wall of ice keeps the water from running off. The moon is lit from within, and stars are nothing more than small, bright disks. He offered $5,000 to anyone who could convince him otherwise. Voliva never paid out, and he explained why: "I have whiped to smitherens any man in the world in a mental battle."

Voliva started the nation's first Christian radio station, WCBD, in 1922. It transmitted an endless stream of snake oil and brimstone that is seldom matched today. On it he predicted he would live to be 120 years old, but he died in 1942 at the age of 72, 48 years short of his forecast. That was the final straw for most of his followers. They'd put up with too much for too long. Anxious to purchase tan shoes, oysters, and pork, the sect dispersed into obscurity.

Zion Historical Society, Shiloh House, 1300 Shiloh Blvd., Zion, IL 60099

(847) 746-2427

Hours: June–August, Saturday–Sunday 2–5p.m. or by appointment

Cost: Adults $1, Kids 50¢

Directions: one block west of Rte. 137, four blocks south of Rte. 173

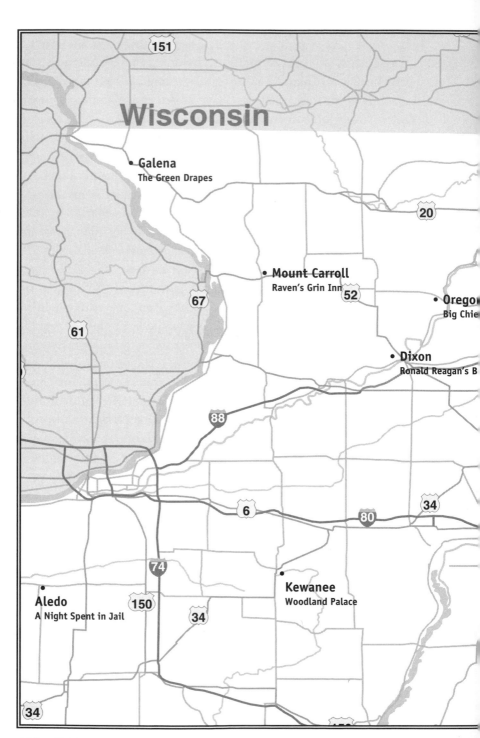

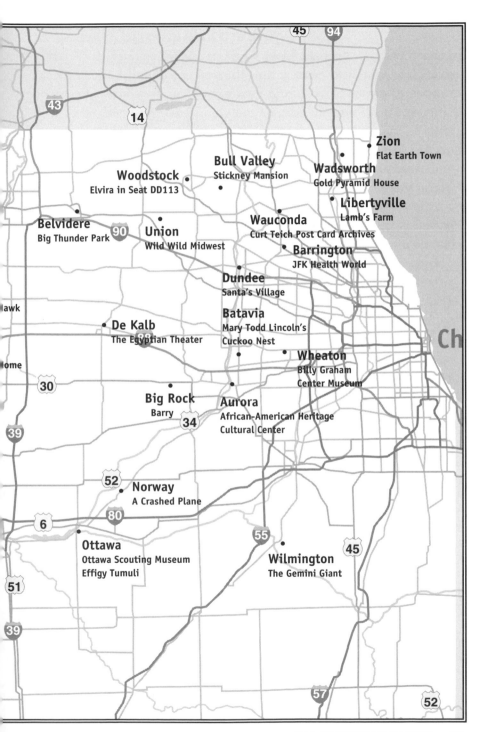

45 94

43

14

Zion
Flat Earth Town

Bull Valley
Woodstock Stickney Mansion **Wadsworth**
Elvira in Seat DD113 Gold Pyramid House

Libertyville
Lamb's Farm
Belvidere **Wauconda**
Big Thunder Park 90 **Union** Curt Teich Post Card Archives
Wild Wild Midwest **Barrington**
JFK Health World
Dundee
Santa's Village
lawk
Batavia
• **De Kalb** Mary Todd Lincoln's
The Egyptian Theater Cuckoo Nest

Wheaton
lome Billy Graham
30 Center Museum

Big Rock
Barry **Aurora**
34 African-American Heritage
39 Cultural Center

52
• **Norway**
A Crashed Plane
80
6

55
Ottawa 45
Ottawa Scouting Museum **Wilmington**
51 Effigy Tumuli The Gemini Giant

39

57 52

4

CeNtraL iLLiNOiS

Central Illinois is Lincoln Country. Lincoln statues. Lincoln hotels. Lincoln outhouses. That's right, when Abe's Springfield privy was excavated several years ago, its contents were big news: a broken chamber pot, two dolls' heads, buttons, glass marbles, toothless combs, and other assorted junk. That's news around here.

But the region is weirder than that. Much weirder. The agrarian society that formed the character of the Great Emancipator now generates folks who bury accordions in elaborate vaults, erect monuments to hippies, and transform Cadillacs into chickenmobiles. And you thought there was nothing between Chicago and St. Louis!

Do you dare? Photo by author, courtesy of Rockome Gardens

Arcola
Rockome Gardens

Rockome Gardens is America's only Amish amusement park. Sound like a contradiction in terms? Perhaps you should pay a visit; it's not all fudge-making and buggy rides.

Strolling around the grounds, you might think somebody has been spiking the apple butter. Six-foot-tall concrete toadstools grow between the pools of lily pads in the Water Garden. For a quarter, in the barn, a trained chicken will challenge you to a game of tic-tac-toe . . . and proba-bly win! A piano-playing skeleton pounds the ivories in the Haunted

Cave while a stuffed, one-eyed calf gazes on. And everywhere you look are fences, planters, birdhouses, and monuments built of broken glass, pottery, old Fresca® bottles, and lots and lots of cement. The stunning gardens are filled with small placards with quaint Amish observations like, "It takes two to make a marriage—the eligible girl and her anxious mother," and "The best garden club is a hoe handle."

If you only want to step back in time, Rockome Gardens has plenty of quilting demonstrations, candle dippers, and goats at the petting zoo. You can cut a log at the horse-power buzz saw and have it branded at the blacksmith shop, all for $1. Or just snap photos of the stern-faced bearded and bonneted employees—it's all part of the fun!

Rockome is a one-of-a-kind place, at least for now. A plan has been announced for Amishland Acres, another Old World amusement park to be built near Tuscola. Will the competition force Rockome Gardens to jump from the 19th to the 21st century, just to stay viable? Don't count on it. They like things just the way they are, or were.

Rte. 133, PO Box 600, 125 N. County Rd. 425 East, Arcola, IL 61910

(217) 268-4106

Hours: May–August, daily 9A.M.–5:30P.M.; April, September–October, Saturday–Sunday 9A.M.–5:30P.M.

Cost: Adults $8.50, Seniors(60+) $7.50, Kids(4–12) $6.50

www.rockome.com

Directions: Follow the signs five miles west of town off Rte. 133, then south.

Louis Klein Broom & Brush Museum and the Coffee Cup Collection

Arcola calls itself "The Broom Town," so it's natural to find the nation's only museum dedicated to the broom. Louis Klein has collected more than 1,000 different items used to sweep and brush, though not all of them are made from broom corn. Look over the shoe scrapers and feather dusters, "naughty" toothbrushes in the shape of a woman's body, makeup brushes with doll handles, bunnylike boot cleaners, toilet scrubbers, and other cleaning devices that you'd never expect to see in a display case. To fully celebrate the usefulness of the brush, come during the Broom Corn Festival in September, an annual event to mark the harvest of more sweeping material, and face off in the National Broom Sweeping Contest!

The Welcome Center is also the repository of Arcola's old coffee cup collection. For many years, the owner of Arrol's Drug Store served residents in the same coffee cup each morning. Each person's name was on his or her own mug, so they never had to share. To join the coffee club, you had to be an Arcola resident who'd drank more than 100 cups already, and there had to be an "opening" on the rack. The only way an opening occurred was if somebody died or moved away. When owner Bob Arrol retired, the cups were sent here.

Arcola Depot Welcome Center, 135 N. Oak St., Arcola, IL 61910

(217) 268-4530

E-mail: arcolacc@arcola-il.com

Hours: Sunday–Friday 9A.M.–5P.M., Saturday 9A.M.–3P.M.

Cost: Free

www.arcola-il.org

Directions: West from I-57, turn right just before the railroad tracks.

Johnny Gruelle Raggedy Ann and Andy Museum

After Barbie, she's America's favorite doll: Raggedy Ann. She was created in 1915 by Arcola native Johnny Gruelle after his daughter Marcella died at age 13. Overcome by grief, Gruelle performed self-therapy by sewing an "I Love You" patch on the breast of Marcella's favorite rag doll. He then began writing stories of Raggedy Ann and her brother Andy's adventures. A craze was born.

Until recently, the only monument to Gruelle and his lovable duo was a headstonelike monument near the town depot and a spooky mop-topped children's parade each spring. But in 1999 Joni Gruelle, a descendant of Johnny, opened a museum on Main Street. It contains original manuscripts and items from Gruelle's estate, hundreds of Raggedy Ann toys and books, and a series of wall murals painted by Gruelle in the basement of a fan, recently rescued and transported here.

110 E. Main St., PO Box 183, Arcola, IL 61910

(217) 268-4908

E-mail: joni@raggedyann-museum.org

Hours: Tuesday–Saturday 10A.M.–5P.M., Sunday 1–4P.M.

Cost: Free

www.raggedyann-museum.org

Directions: In the main business district.

Who thought anyone cared?

America's One and Only Hippie Memorial

There are few places in America where you might least expect a memorial to the American Hippie, but here it is. Based loosely on the Vietnam War Memorial, this monument attempts to show the quantum step upward, and back downward, that marked the beginning and end of the Hippie Movement. The piece is the work of the late Bob Moomaw, a man who split his time between Arcola and Michigan. Moomaw was not a hippie, just the town's eccentric artist-in-residence.

The 40-foot-long wall was originally planned for Arcola, but was constructed in Michigan. After Moomaw's death the memorial was falling into disrepair, so friends and family members brought it to Illinois. While folks here seem generally tolerant of the new town attraction, don't expect the Amish folk to tie-dye their black suits any time soon.

175 N. Oak St., Arcola, IL 61910

Hours: Always visible

Cost: Free

Directions: Just north of the train depot welcome center.

Bloomington
Dead Dorothy

Dorothy Gale, heroine of L. Frank Baum's *Wizard of Oz* series, is believed to be named after Dorothy Gage, Baum's late niece. Gage was born on June 11, 1898, and died on November 11 of the same year, and not from injuries sustained in a tornado. Dorothy's mother was the sister of Baum's wife, Maud. The Baums were living in Chicago when Dorothy passed away in Bloomington. Dorothy's original tombstone was recently discovered by a Baum biographer, just before the inscription became obscured by weathering.

Former Munchkin Mickey Carroll heard about the discovery of Gage's grave and decided to donate a new marker. Because Carroll was a stonemason, he engraved it himself. Now her resting place is easy to find.

Also buried in Evergreen Memorial Cemetery are Adlai Stevenson I and Adlai Stevenson II. Presumably, Adlai Stevenson III will also be planted here, along with future Adlais.

Evergreen Memorial Cemetery, 302 E. Miller St., Bloomington, IL 61701

(309) 827-6950

Hours: Daily 8A.M.–4:30P.M.

Cost: Free

Directions: One block east of 1100 S. Main St., in Section 7.

Something for Ethel.

Brimfield
Jubilee Rock Garden

The Jubilee Rock Garden is a prime example of what one person can do with a pile of rocks, a few bags of cement, and plenty of time on his or her hands. Built over many years by Bill Notzke on his dairy farm, the Jubilee Rock Garden is named after a local college. The terraced garden contains simple mosaic images (clubs, diamonds, hearts, and spades) fashioned from different colored quartzes, mica, geodes, and other colorful rocks.

When Bill's wife Ethel died in 1963, he built a Memorial Arch over his driveway entrance. He would light the arch from the inside, but only on Memorial Day and May 14, Ethel's birthday. Bill continued this tradition until his death. The home has since been sold, and the current owners request that you view the arch and garden from the road.

Route 150, Brimfield, IL 61517

Hours: Private property; always visible from the road

Cost: Free

Directions: On Rte. 150 east of town.

Carlock
The Partisan Dead

A long tradition on partisanship once separated this community, especially in death. It all started when Abraham Carlock, the town founder, was buried in the Woodford County Cemetery under a monument that read, "Here Sleeps the Old Democrat." Carlock was a contemporary of Abraham Lincoln and was not at all impressed by the upstart GOP. Local Republicans saw it as a slap in the face, particularly in the Land of Lincoln.

From that point on, Republicans were planted in the new McLean County Cemetery just across the road (and county line). Democrats were buried with Carlock. No third graveyard was ever established for Libertarians, Communists, or Independents, so Ross Perot's puny body won't be welcome here.

Woodford County Cemetery (Democrats), Carlock, IL 61725

Hours: Daily 9A.M.–5P.M.

Directions: North on Church St. three miles, on the left.

McLean County Cemetery (Republicans), Carlock, IL 61725

Hours: Daily 9A.M.–5P.M.

Directions: North on Church St. three miles, on the right.

BLOOMINGTON

McLean Stevenson was born in Bloomington on November 14, 1929. Stevenson, as Colonel Henry Blake, made many references to Bloomington in TV's *M*A*S*H*.

The Shirk Products factory (103 N. Robinson) in Bloomington-Normal is the only place in the world where **Beer Nuts**, also known as Virginia Redskins, are made.

Champaign
John Philip Sousa Library and Museum

Packed away on the second floor of the U of I's Band Building is a fascinating collection of artifacts related to America's favorite march composer: John Philip Sousa. The majority of this collection was a gift from Albert Austin Harding, a friend of Sousa's. It is roughly divided into three parts: Sousa's sheet music, his band's instruments and artifacts, and the personal collection of Herbert Clarke, a cornet soloist and assistant director with Sousa.

The sheet music is of interest mostly to researchers. It contains 71 percent of Sousa's band performance collection, complete with annotations and notes from the band's travels. The library also has the original band parts for *Stars and Stripes Forever*.

The museum's instrument collection will be of more interest to the casual visitor. If you didn't know better, you might think there had been a mix-up or accident when this 240-piece display was assembled. Many of the instruments look slapped together in mismatched combinations. A wrong mouthpiece here. A horn bell bent at a weird angle there. And who ever heard of an octavin, a rothophone, or a sarrusophone? For many reasons, most of these instruments never made it into popular use.

Many of Sousa's personal effects are also on display, including his traveling podium, Cuban cigars emblazoned with his image, band uniforms, a musical typewriter, a set of backfire brass used at the Battle of Bull Run, and a pewter ship that doubled as a decanter.

Finally, you'll see the personal collection of Herbert Clarke. He was a soloist with Sousa for many years and willed his musical attic to the U of I on his death, expanding the scope of the Sousa collection from a band member's point of view.

236 Harding Band Building, MC-524, 1103 S. 6th St., Champaign, IL 61820

(217) 244-9309

E-mail: p-danner@uiuc.edu

Hours: Monday–Friday 9A.M.–Noon, 1–4P.M.

Cost: Free

www.library.uiuc.edu/sousa

Directions: On the Campus

CHAMPAIGN
Bow-tied columnist **George Will** was born in Champaign on May 4, 1941.

Aieeeee! He's loose!

Charleston
World's Biggest
Abe Lincoln

When you first see it, you have to rub your eyes. Trapped in an abandoned campground east of Charleston, like a presidential Godzilla, is the largest, scariest, most menacing-looking Abe Lincoln ever created. His left hand clutches the Emancipation Proclamation. His right fist is upraised to crush any foe. And though weather-worn and in need of a paint job, he could still put up a good fight against Gamara, should the need arise.

Sadly, this roadside oddity is hundreds of yards from the closest viewing point. But because he is six stories tall and has a head the size of a bus, you can still see him from the road or from the bleachers around an adjoining race car track. If Spring Haven Campground ever reopens, give them your support, for Abe's sake. We don't want to make him angry . . .

Spring Haven Campground (closed), Route 16, Charleston, IL 61920

Hours: Private property; view from the road

Cost: Free

Directions: Just east of town on Rte. 16, behind the raceway along the Embarras River.

If you think President Lincoln's assassination was a crummy payback from a reunified nation, wait until you hear what happened to the Great Emancipator *after* he was murdered.

In Washington, Lincoln's blood was drawn and placed in a ceremonial vessel. According to reports, his brain was "scooped out," reflecting the embalming practice of the day. By removing most of the soft, squishy organs, such as the brain, from the body, the rest would keep pretty well. This was handy if somebody wanted to view the body later. (Lincoln's son Willie, who died in Washington and was prepared in this manner, was twice disinterred so Abe could gaze at and touch the body!) Exactly what happened to Lincoln's brain is not known; it has never been recovered, but you can bet some American family has a doozie of an heirloom.

Lincoln's body rode to Springfield in the first Pullman sleeping car, stopping in many cities along the way. Willie's body rode along with him. Every year, a ghost of Lincoln's funeral train is reported to travel its original path, draped in black bunting and not making a sound.

By the time the funeral train pulled into Springfield, a $50,000 tomb had been erected downtown. But Mary Todd threatened to take Abe back to Washington if she didn't get him planted in Oak Ridge, so Lincoln was placed in a temporary vault and the original tomb was dismantled. Abe was transferred to a more permanent, temporary vault in December, along with Willie and Edward, a son who had died in Springfield at age three.

The three Lincolns stayed in the vault until 1871 when they were moved to the partially completed monument. Just before they were to be placed in the tomb, Lincoln's son Thomas (nicknamed Tad because he had a large head and a wiggly body) died of tuberculosis in Chicago. Thomas was the first Lincoln buried in the Oak Ridge tomb. The monument was dedicated in 1874.

After all the bodies were moved to their new homes, the Big Jim Kinealy Gang, a band of counterfeiters, tried to steal Abe on Election Day, 1876, for a $200,000 ransom. Authorities foiled the plot, but not before the gang yanked Lincoln's casket halfway out of the

sarcophagus. They planned to sink the body in a sandbar beneath a bridge on the Sangamon River two miles north of town, then use the ransom to free Benjamin Boyd, their jailed engraver.

The events caused the monument's builders to reconsider their original design. The next time they would bury Abe deeper and make it look as if he was somewhere else. Before the changes could be made, Abe was moved to a mystery location inside the tomb, known only to the "Lincoln Guard of Honor." The public was left to gaze at an empty sarcophagus they thought contained the former President. Lincoln was hidden for 11 years and was shuffled around several times before being buried under the floor with Mary Todd.

In 1899, it was necessary to reconstruct the tomb due to its shoddy original design. Before Abe was buried a third time, his coffin was opened for 23 old friends and associates to confirm that Lincoln was still dead and still there. He was both. Those present claimed Abe had weathered the years well but had gotten quite stinky. God only knows what he'd have smelled like had his brain been left in.

When repairs were finished in 1901, Lincoln was planted in a reinforced concrete chamber below the sarcophagus with a 20-inch cement slab between the two. Mary Todd Lincoln was re-entombed above ground in a wall chamber opposite the President along with their three sons. (Son Robert was never buried with the rest of the family, but in Arlington National Cemetery.)

Lincoln's tomb became a popular tourist destination and soon resembled a sideshow. Caretakers were allowed to charge admission to supplement their meager salaries, and one caretaker, the enterprising former newsman Herbert W. Fay, placed his 30,000-piece collection of Lincoln memorabilia in the monument's rotunda. You could view Abe's vessel of blood (a placard read, "Lincoln's blood, ask how it came here."), admire bronze statues covered in house paint, or get a local schoolchild to recite the Gettysburg Address for a quarter.

Again, in 1930, repairs were needed. Parts of the external statuary had been nabbed by souvenir hunters, including sabers from the soldiers' hands and telescopes from the sailors', and had to be replaced.

HONEST ABE IN A SHELL GAME

The sarcophagus that once held Lincoln's body (up until the counterfeiters tried to nab him) was left outside the tomb, where visitors hacked it up for keepsakes. In an attempt to cover their own negligence, tomb caretakers dumped the few remaining fragments between two interior walls, where they gathered dust until being discovered in 1979. The obelisk was reinforced, but not before wind knocked over a 100-foot scaffold holding its three-ton capstone which nearly smashed through the tomb's roof. Abe, Mary, and the sons were moved to four different mausoleums in an elaborate shell game on the grounds of Oak Ridge during the project's final phases. Nobody was told they had been moved to discourage vandals.

The tomb continues to have its problems. It was desecrated in 1987 by local teenagers who claimed they had nothing better to do. The kids were caught after police read the vandals' names, which they had spray painted on the side of the structure.

Several years ago scientists asked to drill into Abe's coffin for tissue samples. They wanted to test his DNA for Marfan's Syndrome, a genetic disease believed to be responsible for his lanky frame. The request was denied. Conspiracy wackos wondered out loud if the scientists would try to clone him like the dinosaurs in *Jurassic Park*.

CLINTON

It was in front of the Clinton Courthouse on July 27, 1858, that **Abraham Lincoln** made his famous observation, "You can fool all of the people part of the time and part of the people all of the time, but you cannot fool all of the people all of the time." A statue now marks the spot.

EUREKA

Ronald Reagan attended Eureka College (300 E. College) and played on the football team. He lived in the Tau Kappa Epsilon House and graduated in the class of 1932.

Dahinda
Sleep in a Barn

Barns have long been "hobo hotels," but you don't have to be a bum to stay in this one—it's a bed and breakfast! And as barns go, this is one of the nicest around, complete with pool table, claw-foot tub, outdoor shower, a kitchen in the horse stall, and no TV. What could be more relaxing? The Barn sits on a 150-acre working farm along the Spoon River and is a perfect getaway for hiking, fishing, or doing absolutely nothing. The hayloft sleeps up to nine and is only rented to one group a night, so you won't be bunking with strangers.

And don't worry that this place might smell like an old barn; it has never been used to house animals. It was built in 1993 as a guest house for the owners' children and grandchildren, but at their friends' suggestions, the couple started renting it as a B&B. It was constructed using traditional methods from timbers cut on the farm and 700 hand-carved wooden pegs. Only the floorboards are held down with antique square nails. The space is homey and comfortable, both air-conditioned and heated depending on the season. If you'd like to build a bonfire, there's a place for that, too.

The Barn B&B, PO Box 92, 1690 Kenny St., Dahinda, IL 61428
(309) 639-4408
E-mail: miked@biddersandbuyers.com
Hours: January–November; call ahead for reservations
Cost: $60 single, $70 double, $35 for each additional guest up to seven
www.bbonline.com/il/thebarn/
Directions: One-half mile west of the Dahinda post office, at the end of the road.

Danville
Celebrity Way

Did you know several celebrities hail from Danville? Don't feel bad; most people don't. That's why the town constructed Celebrity Way, a sidewalk tribute to famous Danvillians.

Dick Van Dyke

Dick Van Dyke graduated from Danville High in 1944 where he was Junior Class President. One of his first jobs was as a radio announcer on local station WDAN. (Star at Vermilion & Voorhees Sts.)

Jerry Van Dyke

Dick's younger brother Jerry was born in Danville July 27, 1931. He was the only Van Dyke to return; in a few of many years between *My Mother the Car* and *Coach*, he lived on Logan Avenue across from the Danville Tennis Club. (Star at Vermilion & Fairchild Sts.)

Donald O'Connor

Best known as the third wheel in *Singin' in the Rain*, O'Connor also played the main human role in *Francis the Talking Mule*. (Star at Vermilion St. & Liberty Lane.)

Gene Hackman

Hackman once worked as a staff artist for a local TV station, but broke into acting after leaving Illinois. (Star at Vermilion St. & Lake Shore Dr.)

Bobby Short

This famous lounge crooner was born in Danville in 1924. (Star at Gilbert & Fairchild Sts.)

Celebrity Way also has stars dedicated to accomplished residents with less name recognition, such as astronaut Joe Tanner, footballer Zeke Bratkowski, and Uncle Joe Cannon, former Speaker of the U.S. House of Representatives.

Visitors Bureau, 100 W. Main St., Suite 146, Danville, IL 61832

(800) 383-4386

E-mail: dacvb@soltec.net

Hours: Always visible

Cost: Free

www.danvillecvb.com

Directions: Most celebrity signs off Rte. 1.

DANVILLE

Each June, Danville holds daylong Turtle Races at the Eastern Illinois Fairgrounds.

Part chicken. Part Caddy.

Decatur and Springfield
Krekel's Kustard and the Chicken Cadillacs

If you're planning a quick bite in Decatur or Springfield, stop by the weirdest burger joints in these towns: Krekel's Kustard. Parked outside these two average-looking eateries are 1970s Cadillacs converted into fabulous Chickenmobiles, complete with rooster tails and six-foot, red-eyed heads. The cars are hard to miss, which is exactly the point. If the Chicken Cadillacs don't attract you, you should also know their burgers beat Big Macs hands-down.

There are five Krekels in Decatur and one in Springfield. The Cadillacs are only at the Springfield location and the Decatur Rte. 36 location.

Decatur Location, 2310 E. Main (Rte. 36), Decatur, IL 62521

(217) 423-1719

Springfield Location, 2121 N. Grand East, Springfield, IL 62702

(217) 525-4952

Hours: Monday–Saturday 10:30A.M.–8:30P.M.

Cost: Meals $2–$5

Decatur
Haunted Greenwood Cemetery

Ever since the Sangamon River overflowed through this cemetery in the late 1800s, things haven't been the same. The flood caused a mudslide that unearthed, washed away, and scattered caskets and skeletons of Civil War soldiers. Confederate prisoners, some of whom might have been buried alive during a yellow fever outbreak, were mixed together with Union soldiers, and worse yet, might have been reburied beneath Yankee tombstones. Since then, strange ghost lights have been seen on the hill in the southwest corner of the cemetery.

People have also spotted the spirits of eight Native Americans murdered here in the 1820s. Moonshiners killed them in the Hell Hollow corner of the graveyard. Other people have reported seeing a spook with holes instead of eyes. And still others have bumped into the Greenwood Bride, a ghostly woman who committed suicide after the murder of her fiancé.

Greenwood Cemetery is a beautiful Victorian cemetery, but be careful if you visit, even during the daytime. Rumors have long circulated that crumbling tunnels lie just beneath the surface. They have been known to swallow up caskets . . . and perhaps snoopy visitors.

Greenwood Cemetery, 606 S. Church St., Decatur, IL 62522

(217) 422-6563

Hours: Daily 9A.M.–5P.M.

Cost: Free

www.prairieghosts.com/greenwd1.html

Directions: Nine blocks south of Rte. 36, two blocks west of Business 51.

CUBA
Because it is surrounded by ponds, the founders of Cuba named the village after an island.

GALESBURG
George Gale Ferris, inventor of the Ferris wheel, was born in Galesburg on February 14, 1859.

Poet **Carl Sandburg** was born in Galesburg (331 E. 3rd) on January 6, 1878. It is also here, behind this home, that his ashes were interred beneath a red granite boulder, Remembrance Rock.

But what if it melts?

East Peoria
Twistee Treat's Giant Cone

These prefab fiberglass ice cream stands used to be a common site on American highways. Today only a few remain. The two-story Giant Ice Cream Cone is a vanilla soft serve atop a flat-bottomed sugar cone. The grills and the ice cream machines are located in the cone, but the seating area is in a small building attached in the rear. Twistee Treat serves a standard fast-food fare, but dipped cones are their specialty.

Twistee Treat, 1207 E. Washington St., East Peoria, IL 61611

(309) 699-2604

Hours: Daily 11A.M.–10P.M.; cone always visible

Cost: Small Cone $1, Medium $1.25, Large $1.50

Directions: On Washington St. (Rte. 8) and Leadley Ave., north of I-74.

I'll take the one on top. Photo by James Frost

Gays Double-Decker Outhouse

A double-decker outhouse sounds like a bad idea, but it works. When it was built in 1869, this structure backed up to a general store with an apartment above it. Residents on the second floor could unload their burdens without coming downstairs, and store customers had their own facility below. Both levels had a two-seater, so the facility could accommodate four at a time.

How did it work? Waste from above dropped to the pit behind a false wall; the bottom poopers didn't need to dodge any gifts from above. Still, imagine their nervousness at hearing footsteps above their heads.

The apartment and general store have been torn down, and only the outhouse remains. This makes for a fantastic photo opportunity: "Here we are at an Illinois Rest Area."

1022 Front St., Gays, IL 61928

Hours: Always visible

Cost: Free

Directions: Just north of the grain elevator off Rte. 16.

Hitler's Bicycle

At first you want to believe it. Here, in the middle of nowhere, around the corner from a double-decker outhouse, is a rusted bicycle hanging on a pole and labeled "Hitler's Bike (1934)." It *looks* old enough. Could it have been smuggled back to the states by a souvenir-hungry GI? Perhaps.

But was Hitler even the bike-riding type? On closer inspection you realize the bike is only held on with baling wire. The hand-lettered sign looks like something out of Li'l Rascals. If you start asking questions of local residents, you'll learn that it was put up by the town prankster. Why spend money on a Visitors Bureau when an old bike will draw in the city slickers just as easily?

1110 Front St., Gays, IL 61928

Hours: Always visible

Cost: Free

Directions: Just west of the outhouse.

Lincoln
Lincoln-Mania

Lincoln, Illinois, is the only town in the nation named for Abraham Lincoln while he was still alive. In fact, it was named Lincoln before Abe was elected to national office. Lincoln was an up-and-coming lawyer who was called upon in 1853 to draft the town's incorporation papers. He responded to the founders' name suggestion with unlawyerly humility, "I think you are making a mistake. I never knew anything named Lincoln that ever amounted to much."

Lincoln presided over the town's dedication celebration on August 27, 1853. The official story says he poured out the juice from a watermelon to christen the ground, but another story claims he spit out a mouthful of watermelon seeds in a vulgar gesture! A statue has been erected near the train station where it all took place. The statue isn't of Lincoln. It's of the watermelon.

Watermelon Statue, 101 N. Chicago St., Lincoln, IL 62656

(217) 732-8687

Hours: Always visible

Cost: Free

Directions: At Broadway, near the railroad depot.

Mattoon
The Mad Gasser of Mattoon

Beware the Mad Gasser of Mattoon—he could still be on the loose! On the evening of September 1, 1944, a local couple was overcome by a sweet odor that made their lips swell, their bodies go numb, and their vision blur. A local snoop reported seeing a man in a tight-fitting black suit, skull cap, and gas mask hanging around the couple's home. Before long, rumors of a mysterious attacker swept the city, fanned in part by the Mattoon *Daily Journal-Gazette*. Each night more people were overcome by whiffs of gas that sent "electric shocks" through their bodies. The resulting paralysis prevented the victims from running for help. Investigators found mysterious damp rags and empty lipstick tubes and sent them to chemists for analysis, yet nothing out of the ordinary was ever discovered. Doctors attributed the illnesses to "war nerves" and lack of sleep.

But Mattoon residents weren't buying their explanations. They formed shotgun-wielding posses to patrol the streets, but the "escaped lunatic" was never caught. Paranormal experts claimed it was Spring Heel Jack, a phantom gasser who had terrorized London a century earlier. How he had lived so long, and why he resurfaced in Mattoon, wasn't known.

Two weeks later, when attention returned to World War II, the gassings ceased. The final "victim" was the town's only fortuneteller. She cornered the Mad Gasser in her house and claimed he looked like an ape man.

Psychologists today claim the Mad Gasser of Mattoon is a classic case of American mass hysteria, on par with the Salem Witch Trials and the *War of the Worlds* radio broadcast. No evidence was ever produced that anyone ever attacked the people of Mattoon—they did it to themselves.

Chamber of Commerce, 1701 Wabash Ave., Mattoon, IL 61938

(217) 235-5661

Hours: When you least expect it

Cost: Free

Directions: All over the northwest side of town.

MACOMB
UFOs were spotted over Macomb for almost a week during early August 1998. Bright, yellow lights would appear, disappear, and be chased by military jets, according to reports.

McLean
Route 66 Hall of Fame Museum

The Dixie Trucker's Home has been operating on Route 66 since 1928, so it's the perfect spot to honor The Mother Road. This small museum, open since 1990 and located behind the diner and gift shop, is short on artifacts and big on nostalgia. They've got a can of Anheuser-Busch's "Root 66" root beer, the nameplate from a Tucker automobile, a WPA brush hog, and lots of photos of people you'd probably never recognize. Most are Illinois residents who have made Illinois's stretch of Route 66 what it is today (or was yesterday). Officially, Route 66 was decertified on June 27, 1985, and only exists as a modern historical trail.

The truck stop in which the museum resides has been closed for only one day since it opened seventy years ago—after it burned to the ground in 1965. The pumps opened the next day and the restaurant was rebuilt. The food is good, especially by truck stop standards, and the gift shop is full of Route 66 memorabilia.

Dixie Trucker's Home, Rte. 136, McLean, IL 61754

(309) 874-2323

Hours: Open 24 hours

Cost: Free

www.illinois66.com

Directions: Off I-55 at Rte. 136.

Route 66 Association of Illinois, 2743 Veterans Parkway, Room 166, Springfield, IL 62704

Monmouth
Wyatt Earp's Birthplace

Wyatt Berry Stapp Earp's family lived so many places in Monmouth it's difficult to determine where he was actually born. The owners of this small home are confident that it was here, in the home of his aunt, where the gunslinging baby drew his first breath on March 19, 1848. They've got several notarized affidavits from descendants posted on the walls, each saying something like, "I am the third cousin twice removed from Wyatt Earp's uncle, and he told me that 406 S. Third St. was where Wyatt was born." Though Wyatt might have been born here, it was not where his family lived. Their addresses included 125 N. First St. and 409–411 S. B St., among other locations.

Being just a child, Earp didn't earn much of a shoot-em-up reputation until after he left Illinois. In fact, when he lived in Monmouth he once *hid* at the corner of Third Street and Archer Avenue from a group of Indians. Yellow-bellied coward! Still, the city of Monmouth has erected a monument to Earp in the Monmouth City Park.

Wyatt Earp Birthplace, 406 S. Third St., Monmouth, IL 61462

(309) 734-6419

E-mail: wyattearpbpmel@webtv.net

Hours: May–August, Sunday 1–4P.M.; OK Corral Show 2P.M., 3P.M.

Cost: $3

www.misslink.net/misslink/earp.htm

Directions: Three blocks east and four blocks south of the town square.

Monmouth City Park, Monmouth, IL 61462

Hours: Sunrise–sunset

Cost: Free

Directions: Off Rte. 164 at 11th St., near the airport at the northeast end of town.

Do you see it?

Quincy
Jesus in a Tree

Seeing isn't necessarily believing, but seeing can still be creepy, even if you don't believe. Near the center of this otherwise humdrum cemetery is a large tree with a seven-foot burl on its trunk. If you look at it just right, from a distance, you can make out the figure of Jesus carrying a lamb in his folded arms. Reading bark is about as precise as reading tea leaves, so for all anyone knows, it could be a dead band member from Lynyrd Skynyrd.

The Apparition Tree was first noticed in July 1998 and was visited by thousands of curious folk each day. Today, ropes mark paths to keep visitors from trodding on the dead. The best view is from a distance, but unblocked sightlines are often difficult through the throngs of the faithful.

Calvary Cemetery, 1730 N. 18th St., Quincy, IL 62301

(217) 223-3390

Hours: Daily 9A.M.–5P.M.

Cost: Free

Directions: North of Rte. 104, west of Rte. 96.

Villa Katherine.

Villa Katherine

Villa Katherine looks like it would be more at home in Tunisia than in the Corn Belt, but here it is. The castle was commissioned in 1900 by George Metz and was constructed and furnished with scraps of Moorish architecture scavenged during Metz's two-year trek through North Africa, including lamps, tiles, keyhole windows, crescent ornaments, and more. Metz named the building after his mother, then went in search of a bride.

But having the grooviest pad in Quincy didn't impress his German girlfriend; she refused to leave her homeland, no matter how fabulous his place was. Metz returned to Villa Katherine to live as a recluse with his dog Bingo.

Disheartened, Metz eventually sold the place to a railroad agent in 1912. The buyer had misrepresented his motives, and rather than keep the place pristine, he sold its furnishings and slated the building for demolition. Metz visited Villa Katherine in 1913 to find it vacant and vandalized. He turned away and never came back. Metz occupied the remainder of his life feeding the squirrels and birds in Quincy parks. He died in 1937.

Luckily, the railroad never razed the structure. Villa Katherine sat empty until the 1980s when funds were collected to restore it. Today it houses the local visitor's bureau and is listed on the National Register of Historic Places.

532 Gardner Expressway, PO Box 732, Quincy, IL 62301

(217) 224-3688

Hours: Monday–Saturday 9A.M.–5P.M., Sunday 1–5P.M.

Cost: Adults $2, Kids(5–12) $1

Directions: Overlooking the Mississippi River off Rte. 57 south of the bridge.

Hee Haw Pickup

The *Hee Haw* Pickup is not as famous as the *Beverly Hillbillies'* truck, but it runs a close second. It's the crown jewel of this 35-car museum, and they don't take it out for just any occasion. You can see it at the car club's annual Father's Day show and during the few hours they're open each summer. If you're a true *Hee Haw* fan, you'll make the effort.

Given the number of cornball jokes uttered in the front seat of this bumpkin-mobile, you might think this thing runs on ethanol. Not true. Leaded gas works fine.

Mississippi Valley Historic Automobile Club Antique Car Museum, All-American Park, Quincy, IL 62301

(217) 656-3791

Hours: May–September, Sunday 11A.M.–4P.M.

Cost: Adults $1, Kids 50¢

Directions: At the corner of Front and Cedar, down by the river.

Lincoln-Douglas Valentine Museum

No, Abraham Lincoln and Steven Douglas did not send each other valentines. There's no indication that they even liked one another. The name of this tiny museum of candy boxes is drawn from the building that houses the collection: the Lincoln-Douglas Apartments.

Covering the walls of the communal library in this senior high-rise is an interesting assortment of heart-shaped containers. The Quincy Paper Box Company manufactured valentine candy boxes for years, and they donated their production samples to create the museum when the plant closed. Residents have expanded the collection by adding other items related to the holiday. Though the collection takes only a few short minutes to view, it's worth a visit if you're in Quincy.

Lincoln-Douglas Apartments, 101 N. 4th St., Quincy, IL 62301

(217) 224-3355

Hours: Monday–Friday 9A.M.–9P.M. by appointment

Cost: Free

Directions: At the corner of Maine and 4th Sts.

Rantoul
Octave Chanute Aerospace Museum

When you first enter the Chanute Aerospace Museum, you'll swear you've just walked into a boy's bedroom. Plastic model airplanes battle each other in crude dioramas. The walls are covered in poorly painted renderings of cartoon characters dropping bombs and tossing thunderbolts. But this isn't some preteen hell—it's an old air force base! When the federal government handed the folks in Rantoul a decommissioned lemon, they made tourist lemonade.

Check out the Commander's Office with its original desk and carpeting. Visit the hangers filled with rusting jets and missiles. Hop in the cockpit of a B-52 or a C-130 transport and, as a promotional flyer says, "Remember living on the brink of destruction as huge C-133 Douglas Cargomasters transported ICBMs and their nuclear payloads to launching sites around the midwest."

During the Cold War, Chanute Air Force Base was a primary training ground for Minuteman missile repair teams. The three trainers are now open for you to visit and inspect, whether you be a red-blooded

American or a red-blooded Red. Imagine launching ICBMs at all those who ever wronged you!

The irony of an aerospace museum at Chanute is lost on some, but not those who served in WWII. At the time, Chanute was akin to Siberian for washed-out or washed-up pilots. Among servicemen, the common phrase was "Don't shoot 'em, Chanute 'em!"

Chanute Air Base, Grissom Hall/Hanger 4, 1011 Pacesetter Dr., PO Box 949, Rantoul, IL 61866-0949

(217) 893-1613

Hours: Monday–Friday 10A.M.–5P.M., Saturday 10A.M.–6P.M., Sunday Noon–5P.M.

Cost: Adults $5, Seniors(62+) $4, Kids(4–17) $3

www.cu-online.com/~leonhard/chanute/

Directions: Exit 250 (Rte. 136) from I-57, travel east to Rte. 45, turn south to museum.

Salisbury
Colin Folk Art

If you drive too fast through Salisbury, don't blink, or you'll miss one of the finest folk artists in the state. Tucked away in a small gallery building is Colin Folk Art, a central Illinois gem.

George Colin has been making folk art for many years, starting first on painted wood and moving on to pastels. His painted wood pieces are mostly intended for outdoor display, but they aren't the typical lawn butts and kissing Dutch children. More likely you'll find Elvis on a lounge chair, purple corn stalks, or alligators snapping at passersby. His bright pastels now hang in the Governor's Mansion and the homes of Oprah and Michael Jordan.

Half the fun of visiting Colin Folk Art is chatting with George's wife and business manager, Winnie. She has an opinion or anecdote about any topic you might bring up, from the price of tea in China to Washington's most recent political scandal. Be sure to throw out random topics as you dig through George's work. She will keep you entertained.

Route 97, Salisbury, IL 62677

(217) 626-1204

Hours: Call ahead

Cost: Free

Directions: Just west of the town tavern.

Springfield
Oliver Parks Telephone Museum

Oliver Parks worked as a lineman for Illinois Bell for 40 years, and in that time he collected lots of phones, cable, and insulator caps. When Parks retired he asked the phone company if it wanted to display his collection, and it did. The result is the Oliver Parks Telephone Museum, housed in the ground floor of Springfield's Ameritech offices.

The most stirring exhibit in the collection is a salute to the brave linemen. Guess who's most prominently featured? One hint: it's not Glen Campbell! From crank phones to Swinglines, rotaries to Touch-Tones™, they've got them all.

529 S. 7th St., Springfield, IL 62701

(217) 789-5303

Hours: Monday–Friday 8A.M.–5P.M.

Cost: Free

www.springfield-il.com/tourism/phonemus.html

Directions: Across from the Lincoln Home Visitors Center.

Birthplace of the Corn Dog

Corn dogs were originally called Cozy Dogs. At the Cozy Dog Inn in Springfield, they still are. The cornbread-dipped, deep-fried wieners were introduced to the American people in 1949 by Ed Waldmire along Old Route 66. Ed had perfected his recipe while living in Amarillo, Texas, during WWII, calling it the "Crusty Cur." Waldmire renamed it the "Cozy Dog" at his wife's suggestion before opening his Illinois store.

Cozy Dogs were an instant hit, and imitations soon followed. Ripoffs were given a more generic name—corn dogs—and the name stuck . . . at least outside of Springfield. The Cozy Dog Inn has a faithful local following, with good reason. Those who did them first still make them best.

The Cozy Dog Inn was recently remodeled to accommodate more customers. It still sits on Old Route 66, an honor it celebrates with a display of 1950s roadside memorabilia.

Cozy Dog Inn, 2935 S. 6th St., Springfield, IL 62703

(217) 525-1992

Hours: Monday–Saturday 8A.M.–8P.M.

Cost: $1.35 each, plus tax

Directions: On the south side of town on Business 55.

One more indignity.

Abraham Lincoln's Tomb

Though most days Lincoln's tomb has an aura of solemnity, this memorial has been the site of many strange events over the years, most of them involving the body of the President. When you view Lincoln's sarcophagus today, you're looking at an empty shell; Abe is actually 13 feet below floor level with a six-foot slab of concrete just above his coffin. This is to discourage grave robbers.

Outside the tomb is a bust sculpted by Gutzon Borglum of Mt. Rushmore fame. Tradition says you should rub Abe's nose for luck. After several years, his nose became a bright, shining beacon on his dull, bronze face. Caretakers tried putting Abe on a pedestal out of tourists' reach, but the public demanded that it be lowered, and it was. So rub away—there's plenty of the slain President's good fortune still left in him.

Oak Ridge Cemetery, 1500 N. Monument Ave., Springfield, IL 62702

(217) 782-2717

Hours: Daily 9A.M.–5P.M. (4P.M. winters)

Cost: Free

www.state.il.us/HPA/LINCTOMB.HTM

Directions: On the north side of town, off North Grand Ave.

A Tomb for Accordions

As you enter Oak Ridge Cemetery you'll see an impressive crypt dedicated to a remarkable man. No, not Abraham Lincoln. Roy Bertelli! Master of the Accordion!

Truth be known, (as of this writing) Bertelli isn't dead, but he's already bought a highly visible plot at the first fork in the road on the way to the Lincoln Tomb. Emblazoned on the front face of his above-ground sarcophagus is an engraved photo of a young Roy playing his favorite instrument. A raised headstone with an open accordion marks the other end of the tomb. On sunny days, Roy sits atop his plot, playing away to the amusement of visitors and the annoyance of locals. They've heard enough.

Because Bertelli is a war veteran, he will be buried with full honors at nearby Camp Butler. But lest anyone forget his contribution to the art of the squeezebox, his accordions will be laid to rest at this Oak Ridge tomb.

Oak Ridge Cemetery, 1500 N. Monument Ave., Springfield, IL 62702

(217) 782-2717

Hours: Daily 9A.M.–5P.M. (4P.M. winters)

Cost: Free

Directions: On the north side of town, off North Grand Ave.

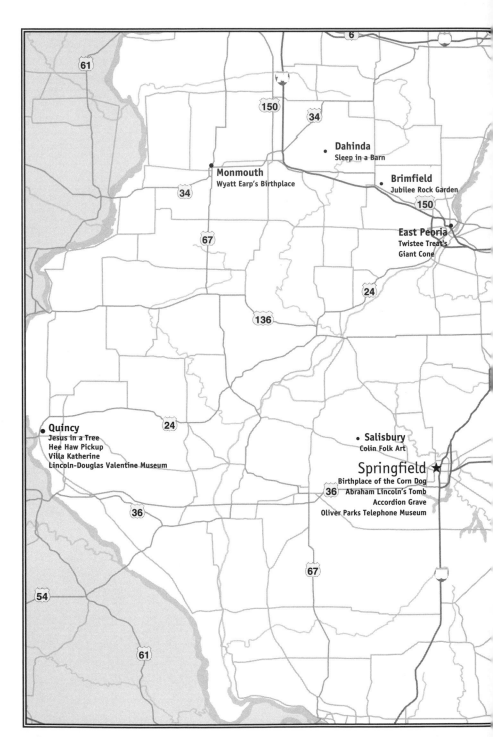

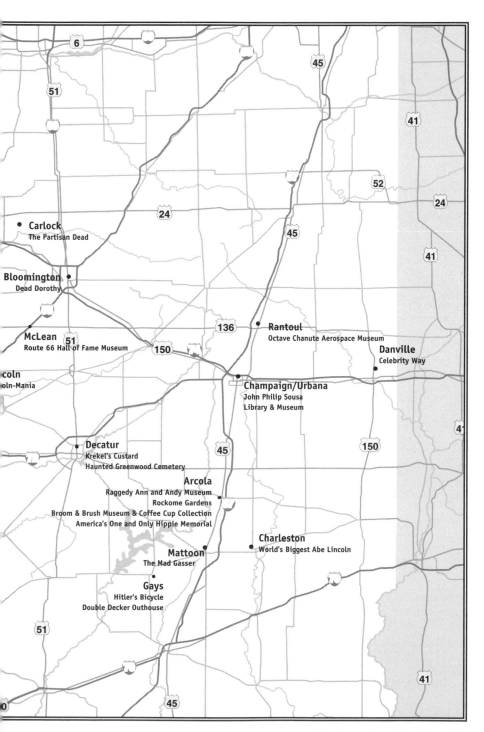

- **Carlock**
  The Partisan Dead

- **Bloomington**
  Dead Dorothy

- **McLean** 51
  Route 66 Hall of Fame Museum

coln
oln-Mania

- **Decatur**
  Krekel's Custard
  Haunted Greenwood Cemetery

Arcola
Raggedy Ann and Andy Museum
Rockome Gardens
Broom & Brush Museum & Coffee Cup Collection
America's One and Only Hippie Memorial

Mattoon
The Mad Gasser

- **Gays**
  Hitler's Bicycle
  Double Decker Outhouse

Rantoul
Octave Chanute Aerospace Museum

Danville
Celebrity Way

Champaign/Urbana
John Philip Sousa
Library & Museum

Charleston
World's Biggest Abe Lincoln

5

SOUTHERN ILLINOIS

$\mathcal{S}$outhern Illinois, often referred to as "Little Egypt," got its name from the Nile-like delta confluence of the Ohio and Mississippi Rivers, but the region has another Egyptian connection. A local man, Russell Burrows, has claimed he found the tomb of Cleopatra, Mark Antony, Ptolemy, and Alexander the Great in a cave near Salem. But the still-unrevealed "Burrows' Cave" is said to be guarded by ghosts, so don't even try to find it.

Perhaps all the good-natured use of pyramids and pharaohs by local businesses has opened up a portal to another dimension, allowing devil birds and albino squirrels to enter at will. UFOs and crop circles are not uncommon in this region. And if you're traveling to Southern Illinois, you might want to think twice about camping. Bigfoot is no stranger to Little Egypt.

Two Effingham boys first saw the hairy beast in 1912, but it wasn't spotted again until 1941. That year, the Reverend Lepton Harpole was fishing near Mount Vernon when a "baboon" jumped on him from a tree, knocking off Harpole's hat. As the creature ran away, the good reverend realized it was not a baboon, but something much more humanlike.

Sasquatch was sighted three more times, in Chittyville (1968), in Shawnee National Forest (1970) where it clawed at Mike Busby before being scared off by a pickup truck, and in Cairo (1972). Then, in 1974, the monster seemed to settle down around Murphysboro.

But if you think Bigfoot is the only weirdness going on in Little Egypt, think again. There are plenty of bizarre tourist destinations to keep you entertained.

It draws bugs from three different states!

Alto Pass
Bald Knob Cross

Perched atop Bald Knob Mountain near the southern tip of Illinois, Bald Knob Cross lays claim to the title of North America's Tallest Christian Monument. It stands 111 feet tall, is 63 feet wide, and can withstand wind speeds of up to 150 mph. And because it is illuminated at night, it also attracts flying bugs from three different states!

Its outer surface is covered in white, porcelain-coated, metal panels, not unlike a giant refrigerator. This avoids the trouble of having to repaint the cross, and if a big magnetic Jesus is ever found the owners won't need nails to hang him on it.

Bald Knob Cross was built in 1963 by Wayman Presley and Rev. William Lirely. Each white panel was purchased through contributions, like that of Myrta Clutts. Her prize pig Betsy farrowed over 1,700 piglets, all of which were sold for the Cross Fund. You can read this touching story on a flier available in the gift shop (open during the summer).

The best time to visit this mountaintop shrine is on Easter Sunday (6:30 A.M.) when locals put on a sunrise service and Passion Play at an outdoor theater adjoining the cross. If you can't make it, you can always hire Barbara Casey. She has a one-woman puppet show telling the history of Bald Knob Cross and is available for parties and worship services. Check out the Web site.

Route 127, PO Box 100, Alto Pass, IL 62905

(618) 893-2344

Hours: Daily 8 A.M.–6 P.M.

Cost: Free

www.mcleansboro.com/features/baldknob.htm

Directions: Follow the signs west of town from Rte. 127.

Keep your eyes peeled for this critter.

Alton
The Piasa Bird

The Piasa Bird petroglyph was first documented by Father Père Marquette in his 1673 diary, but it had been part of the regional mystical heritage for centuries. People believe it was intended to scare travelers along the Mississippi, or to honor a great bird-human battle, or both.

An Illini legend tells of two Piasa (pronounced PIE-*saw*, Illini for "Bird That Devours Man") Birds that lived in a cave along the river. They were not shy about eating an occasional Indian. So Illini warriors, led by Chief Ouatoga, ambushed and killed the flying varmints using Ouatoga as bait. To commemorate the victory, a Piasa Bird was painted on the bluffs. Native Americans canoeing along the river would fire poisoned arrows, and later guns, at the image.

Stories of a bone-filled cave circulated for years, bolstered by a report from John Russell in March 1836. He claimed to have found a dark recess in the cliffs filled with human skulls and bones. The skeletons were piled so high Russell could not measure their depth.

Nobody made a clear drawing of the original petroglyph, and descriptions varied. Today's best guess looks like ZZ Top's dragon love child with a squared-off beard, deer antlers, and a tail that wraps back past its head. The bullet-ridden Piasa and the caves on the bluffs were carelessly blasted away by European settlers quarrying for lime in 1846.

Local businesses repainted the image in 1925, but it was dynamited in 1950 when McAdams Highway was widened. A Piasa sign was bolted to the cliffs until just a few years ago, but now the image has been painted directly onto the rock face. On either side of the Piasa are entrances to caves that appear to be the gathering places of beer- and devil-worshipping teens. Plans to have the Piasa illuminated at night are in the works.

Great River Road (Rte. 100), Alton, IL 62002

(800) 258-6645

Hours: Always visible

Cost: Free

www.altonweb.com/history/piasabird/index.html

Directions: On the bluffs along Rte. 100, one mile north of the casino.

DOES THE PIASA STILL LIVE?

Despite the Illini victory over the Piasa Bird, some believe the monster still terrorizes people along the Mississippi. Colonel Walter F. Siegmund sighted something odd near Alton on April 24, 1948. He described it as "an enormous bird about the size of a small pursuit plane" flying along the bluffs. Other reports place the Piasa farther north. Two birds with 10-foot wingspans swooped down and carried 10-year-old Marlon Lowe about 35 feet from his Lawndale home on July 25, 1977. His parents frightened the birds away before the 65-pound child became the birds' lunch. The incident so spooked Marlon that his hair turned from red to gray. Three days later, near Lincoln, a farmer saw one of the birds in flight, and on July 30 "Texas John" Huffer of Tuscola took pictures of a Piasa in a local swamp. Finally, a truck driver saw a bird trying to carry a pig over the highway between Delavan and Armington. The bird had an eight-foot wingspan . . . and a heck of an appetite! Skeptics say the birds were just aggressive turkey vultures.

Martyr for Abolition

"As long as I am an American citizen, and as long as American blood runs in these veins, I shall hold myself at liberty to speak, to write, and to publish whatever I please on any subject amenable to the laws of my country for the same." These words were spoken by Reverend Elijah Lovejoy not long before his American blood stopped running in his veins.

Rev. Lovejoy was a persistent advocate of abolition. Three times, proslavery mobs destroyed the press on which Lovejoy printed his antislavery newspaper, *The Alton Observer*, and each time he replaced it. On November 7, 1837, he was shot while guarding his fourth printing press. Lovejoy became a martyr for the abolitionist cause and, in a broader sense, freedom of the press.

A 90-foot monument to Lovejoy now stands in Alton City Cemetery, the state's tallest monument to an Illinois resident. The frame from the destroyed printing press can be seen in the lobby of the *Alton Telegraph*.

Lovejoy Monument, Alton City Cemetery, 1205 E. 5th St., Alton, IL 62002

(618) 462-1617

Hours: Daily 9A.M.–6P.M.

Cost: Free

Directions: Fifth St. at Monument Ave.

Belleville
National Shrine of Our Lady of the Snows

If Disney built Catholic shrines, Our Lady of the Snows would be the Magic Kingdom. This place is B-I-G. Two hundred acres big. It's the largest outdoor Catholic shrine in the United States! Everywhere you turn there's another chapel, prayer bench, or candle-filled grotto. They've also got most of the Bible's memorable scenes carved in marble, tiled in mosaics, or gilded in gold.

Like Disneyland, there's no way to see it all short of a full day, so here are a few highlights to help you bypass the tour groups:

- **The Journey** This multimedia presentation traces the Bible from cover to cover, both Testaments. The show's beginning is the best: Adam and Eve frolic in the Garden of Eden and are banished for munching an apple, all presented through interpretive dance.
- **The Mary Chapel** Check out the ceiling; it's painted to look like the aurora borealis but looks more like a groovy Jerry Garcia tie.

- **The Way of the Cross** You can walk it, but the road is there for a reason. Cruise past the stations in the comfort of your vehicle. Each scene is depicted with full-size statues. The speed limit is 25 mph.
- **The Agony Garden** Contrary to its name, this place is very quiet and peaceful. Bring a picnic lunch.
- **Lourdes Grotto** Why bother going to France with an exact replica right here?
- **The Way of the Lights** After dark, around Christmas, a million light bulbs blind auto-bound pilgrims on their journey toward a final nativity scene. If the Wise Men had had this much help finding the Baby Jesus, they wouldn't have needed to be so wise.

422 S. DeMazenod Dr., Belleville, IL 62223-1094

(800) 533-6279

E-mail: mami@oblatesusa.com

Shrine Hours: Daily 7A.M.–10P.M.; call ahead at Christmas

Center Hours: Daily 7:30A.M.–8P.M.

Cost: Donations encouraged

www.oblatesusa.org

Directions: At the intersection of Rte. 157 and Rte. 15.

SNOWY MARY STOPS BY

If you want to double your excitement on your visit to Our Lady of the Snows, come on the 13th of the month. Since January 1993, always on the 13th, Ray Doiron comes to the Lourdes Grotto to visit with the Virgin Mary. While the Shrine does not endorse these heavenly communications, they do not discourage it.

Doiron claims that Mary comes to him as he says the Rosary. She is often surrounded by light, making everything around her sparkle, while her robes blow in the wind, kind of like Stevie Nicks. The scent of roses is overpowering. Mary hangs out for 45 minutes, speaking slowly so Doiron can remember her message. Though most of her messages are of three types, "Pray, pray, pray!," "Look out for Satan!," and "The rise of one world government is a prelude to the Rapture!," she occasionally tries to explain why there are earthquakes in Japan or floods in the Midwest. For more details, check out the Apparition Web page: www.Apparitions.org/Doiron.html.

Not a yellow submarine.

Benton
Hard Day's Nite

If you're one of those can't-get-enough-of-the-1960s baby boomers, here's a bed and breakfast for you. Located in the former home of George Harrison's sister, Louise Caldwell, Hard Day's Nite will send you on a nostalgic trip to a decade when you cared more about rock 'n' roll than a scratch on your Land Cruiser.

George Harrison actually visited Louise in this house for a month in September 1963, just before the Beatles hit it big in the United States. The band was already a hit in Europe, and Harrison was taking time out to rest before the British Invasion. Ringo was supposed to come along but backed out at the last minute. George's brother Peter came instead. Harrison played a few gigs with The Vests at the Bocce Ball Club in Benton and the VFW Hall 3479 in Eldorado. Rock historians believe these shows to be the first public performances by a Beatle in the United States.

Don't let the name of this cozy B&B fool you; the beds are soft and the hospitality unmatched. You have your choice of the George Room, the Ringo Room, the Paul Room, or the John Room (which is *not* the toilet). The Ringo Room is downstairs, away from the others, as it should be.

Each room has a VCR and all the Beatles' movies are available on video-tape. The common areas are decorated with Beatles memorabilia, including a pullout couch from Louise's NYC apartment on which George once slept and a BOAC (British Airways) travel bag once given to George.

Two of the best artifacts are a pair of framed letters sent to Louise Caldwell by Bud Connell, Director of Programming for KXIK in St. Louis. The first (dated July 31, 1963) politely declined to play a Beatles recording of a Del Shannon song, claiming the remake eliminated it from consideration. Connell closes with, "Perhaps their next release will become Number 1 in the nation . . . we hope so!" Louise apparently wrote back requesting Connell return the band's recording, and Connell snippily responded (in a letter dated November 6, 1963) that it was *Louise's* fault he no longer had it. She should have told him she wanted it back! Per the station's policy, he gave it away at a "personality's public appearance." Always two-faced, Connell closed with "I *do* hope the Beatles have a gigantic stateside hit . . . soon!" He was as prophetic as he was insincere.

113 McCann St., Benton, IL 62812

(618) 438-2328

E-mail: jimchady@midwest.net

Hours: Year round; call ahead for reservations

Cost: $60/night

www.bbonline.com/il/ilbba/members/harddaysnite.html

Directions: East of the courthouse square off Rte. 34, next to the Benton Gymnasium.

The Old Franklin County Jail Museum

Most small-town historical museums are dreary collections of postcards, spinning wheels, and farm machinery. The Old Franklin County Jail Museum is not one of them.

Central to the museum is the history surrounding the hanging of Charlie Birger, Southern Illinois's most notorious bootlegger. For all his faults as a local hoodlum and killer, Birger did some good in the region, not the least of which was to stand up to the KKK-backed law enforcement establishment of the 1920s. Police had been ruthless to immigrant laborers in Southern Illinois, so to them, Birger took on a Robin Hood aura. He was also at the receiving end of the first bomb ever dropped from a plane in the United States. On November 12, 1926, the rival Sheldon Gang bombed Birger's favorite hangout, The Shady Rest in

Harrisburg, from a biplane. A cockfighting pit was blown to pieces, killing an American eagle and a bulldog, but none of Birger's gang.

Birger was arrested for the contract murder of "Fat" Joe Adams, the mayor of West City and a competitive moonshiner. After a lengthy incarceration and trial, Birger was hanged outside the Old Jail on April 19, 1928, before 5,000+ spectators. It was to be the last public execution in Illinois. Birger hired his own photographer to document the event.

The noose used to hang Birger is on display at the museum, as is the jail cell in which he spent his final days and a replica of the portable gallows from which he dangled. The jail stayed in use until 1989 and still has original prisoner graffiti.

Also at the museum are several other themed rooms dedicated to local history. In one is the recreated WFRX 1300 radio station of West Frankfort where a school reporter interviewed George Harrison on the air in 1963. This equipment was the first to broadcast a Beatles record ("From Me to You") in the United States. The museum also has a Coke machine from Main Street in Benton, from which Harrison might have pulled a bottle or two.

Lastly, the museum focuses its attention on several native sons, including John Logan, the Civil War General who founded the Grand Army of the Republic; Doug Collins, former Philadelphia 76er and coach of the Chicago Bulls; and actor John Malkovich.

209 W. Main St., PO Box 1641, Benton, IL 62812

(800) 661-9998

E-mail: fcbureau@accessus.net

Hours: April–September, Tuesday–Friday 9A.M.–3P.M., Saturday 9A.M.–5P.M., Sunday Noon–5P.M.; October–March, closed Sundays

Cost: Suggested donation: Adults $2, Kids $1

www.fctb.com

Directions: West of the courthouse square on Rte. 14 at 6th St.

BELLEVILLE

Buddy Ebsen was born in Belleville on April 2, 1908. His family ran the Ebsen Natatorium and lived at 805 Lebanon Ave.

Put on some pants.

Cairo
The Hewer

Cairo's statue of *The Hewer* in Halliday Park is thought to be one of the nation's greatest nudes. It was carved by George Grey Barnard in 1906 for the St. Louis World's Fair and is of a young man kneeling on the bank of a river. Once described as "[a] vision of man laboring on the shore of a flood hewing and dragging wood to save the people from death and destruction."

That's all fine and good, but would it hurt to put on a pair of pants?

Halliday Park, 950 Washington Ave., Cairo, IL 62914

(618) 734-2737

Hours: Always visible

Cost: Free

Directions: On Rte. 51 (Washington Ave.) between 9th and 10th Sts.

Chester
Popeye Town

Elzie Crisler Segar unveiled Popeye, the famous spinach-eating sailor, in 1929 as a new character in his 10-year-old "Thimble Theater" comic strip. Popeye was fashioned after Frank "Rocky" Fiegel, a local scrapper on the Mississippi River. Popeye was the captain of a voyage taken by Olive Oyl and her brother Castor. At the time, Olive (modeled after rail-thin Chester shopkeeper Dora Paskal) was dating Ham Gravy. Wimpy joined the strip later; he was based on William "Windy Bill" Schuchert, proprietor of the Chester Opera House where Segar once worked as a projectionist.

In Segar's honor, a six-foot "life-size" bronze Popeye statue was erected near the Mississippi River in Segar Memorial Park. The statue has been attacked three times by Blutoish vandals but has stood its ground. Each year, on the weekend after Labor Day, the town throws a Popeye Picnic where the Popeye Fan Club is well represented.

Many Chester establishments have incorporated Popeye, Olive Oyl, and Wimpy into their names and advertising, and you can buy Popeye brand canned spinach at many locations around town. The best of the bunch is Spinach Can Collectibles in Wimpy's . . . er . . . Schuchert's old Opera House.

Popeye Statue, Segar Memorial Park, Chester, IL 62233

(618) 826-2326

Hours: Always visible

Cost: Free

Directions: At the Chester Bridge over the Mississippi River.

Popeye Mural/Fan Club/Spinach Can Collectibles, Old Chester Opera House, 1001 State St., Chester, IL 62233

(618) 826-4567

Hours: Monday–Friday 9:30A.M.–4:30P.M., Saturday 9A.M.–4P.M.

Cost: Free

www.midwest.net/orgs/ace1

Directions: On Chester Square.

CAIRO

Cairo is named after the Egyptian city of the same name, though locals pronounce it "CAY-roh."

Collinsville
Cahokia Mounds

Cahokia Mounds holds the distinction of being the nation's only pre-Columbian urban metropolis. Before St. Louis became the Gateway to the West, Cahokia (just across the river) was the gateway to the north. It was the trade hub in the Mississippi Valley starting around A.D. 700 until its inhabitants, the Hopewell culture, vacated the site around A.D. 1400. More than 120 mounds once covered the region, though only 109 remain. Some of the mounds were destroyed by railroad engineers looking for dirt for train beds.

The focal point of Cahokia is Monk's Mound. It was named for French Trappist monks who built a monastery atop it in the 1700s. It stands 100 feet tall and covers 14 acres—only two pyramids in Mexico are larger. A large stone structure is believed to be at the center of Monk's Mound, though researchers are baffled as to how it got there. While drilling a drainage hole into the mound in 1998, a crew hit a large rock where no stone was supposed to be. Could the Hopewell culture have been masons? Until recently, archeologists believed not. We may never know what this rock is, for there are no plans to excavate the mound.

As impressive as Monk's Mound is, Mound 72 is cooler. Whoever was buried in Mound 72 was a mighty Big Cheese. The guy was laid out in a robe of 36,000 seashells with 400 arrowheads and was "accompanied" by 53 female and 4 male sacrifices, all of them missing their hands and heads! Sadly, the Interpretive Center plays down these tales of human sacrifice. Perhaps the curators need to do a little market research. Ask 100 visitors which is more interesting; a pile of dirt or decapitated human offerings? Isn't it obvious?

The entire site only hints at the size of the city that once stood here since all the wooden shelters on and around the mounds have long since disintegrated.

7850 Collinsville Rd., PO Box 681, Collinsville, IL 62234

(618) 346-5160

Museum Hours: Daily 9A.M.–5P.M.

Park Hours: Daily 8A.M.–6P.M.

Cost: Free

www.medicine.wustl.edu/~mckinney/cahokia/welcome.html

Directions: Exit 24 from I-255 and turn west on Collinsville Rd.

Many tomatoes gave their lives.

World's Largest Catsup Bottle

Towering above the former Brooks Foods Factory, the World's Largest Catsup Bottle seems lonely without the World's Largest Mustard Bottle by its side. The conical tank, built in 1949, is roughly 25 feet wide at the base and is 70 feet tall. It sits atop a 100-foot pedestal and can hold about 100,000 gallons . . . of water. If it were filled with catsup, this tower could satisfy about 26 million burger-eaters with a teaspoon each.

The Bottle's fate was in danger several years ago, but the citizens of Collinsville rallied and restored the landmark in 1995. Today, the locals occasionally celebrate "Catsup Bottle Celebration Day" to raise money for the tower's upkeep and to sing the praises of catsup. Capping the day, children dress up in bottle-shaped costumes and march in the Catsup Parade. With all this enthusiasm, is another condiment tower in the works? Not likely. Brooks Brothers has long since relocated to Indiana.

Old Brooks Food Factory, 800 S. Morrison, Collinsville, IL 62234

(618) 345-5598

Hours: Always visible

Cost: Free

home.stlnet.com/~jimpotts/catsup.htm

Directions: On Morrison Rd. (Rte. 159) south of downtown.

Catsup Bottle Fan Club, PO Box 1108, Collinsville, IL 62234

E-mail: fries@catsupbottle.com

www.catsupbottle.com

Elsah
Mistake House

Barely larger than a two-car garage, the Mistake House on the campus of Principia College is anything but a mistake. The brainchild of Bernard Maybeck, it was originally called the Sample House because it was used to test materials and methods that would be incorporated into other college buildings. On this 1931 structure you can see poured concrete, a thatched roof, a terra cotta tiled roof, brick walls, half timbers, a chimney, a gabled second floor . . . you name it, it's there.

Driving through Principia College you'll see many of the Mistake House's features in practice. Principia is one of the most beautiful college campuses in the state and would be worth a visit even if the Mistake House wasn't there.

Principia College, Elsah, IL 62028

(618) 374-2131

Hours: Building always visible

Cost: Free

www.prin.edu/v1/index.htm

Directions: Adjacent to the chapel along the bluff.

Makanda
Boomer's Grave

Boomer was a faithful hound dog but not very bright. This three-legged pooch was the trusted pet of a local train engineer. Boomer loved to race locomotives, and oftentimes he won. That either says a lot for Boomer or not much for the locomotives.

On September 2, 1859, Boomer ran barking alongside his master's train, trying to warn him to put out a hotbox fire. The dog was so intent on saving the engine that he did not see an upcoming bridge abutment. He ran headlong into the iron bridge and was killed instantly.

Boomer's body was laid to rest beside the railroad tracks by the man he saved. Today, the monument sits next to a basketball court, 300 feet from the deadly abutment. In the dog's honor, a dormitory at nearby Southern Illinois University was named Boomer Hall.

Railroad Depot, Makanda, IL 62958

Hours: Always visible

Cost: Free

Directions: Just east of the railroad tracks, south of the depot.

EAST ST. LOUIS
Gold-medal-winning track star **Jackie Joyner-Kersee** was born in East St. Louis on March 3, 1962.

EDWARDSVILLE
Jackson Browne recorded "Cocaine" and "Shaky Town" at the Edwardsville Holiday Inn, Room 124, for his album *Running on Empty*. It's now a Comfort Inn (3080 S. Rte. 157).

ENFIELD
On April 25, 1972, a "whangdoodle" terrorized local farmer Henry McDaniel. The three-legged, pink-eyed, big-headed monster crawled onto McDaniel's back porch and peered through the screen door. Henry blasted it three times with a shotgun. The whangdoodle fled but returned the next day and remained at a safe distance. Newspapers dubbed the creature "The Enfield Horror."

Mild-mannered bag boy . . . or Man of Steel?

Metropolis
Superman's Hometown

Any true Superfan knows Superman hailed from Smallville, not Metropolis, but the Metropolis Chamber of Commerce didn't let that detail get in its way. After all, they are the only town named Metropolis in the nation, at least according to the U.S. Postal Service. There are plenty of Smallvilles.

During the 1970s, town leaders transformed this sleepy river burg into the Man of Steel's hometown. Today, Superman's image is on street signs (one street is Lois Lane), stop signs, and telephone booths surrounding the town square. And the local paper? The *Metropolis Planet*! Stop by the Chamber's offices and they'll give you a free sample of Kryptonite, though they discourage you from using it to evil ends.

The town's first Superman statue, made of fiberglass, was a bit misshapen and somebody shot its chest with a speeding bullet. A new bronze (not steel?) Superman was commissioned in 1992 and erected next to the courthouse. A storefront Super Museum opened just off the square; it houses one of George Reeve's original TV costumes among other Super Junk.

Every June the town throws a Superman Celebration, the highlight of which is a fake bank robbery called the Superman Drama. The Man of Steel foils the stripe-suited villains and depositors are safe for another year.

Sadly, however, the superhero has not been getting as much attention since riverboat casinos docked at the landing, the most prominent being the Merv Griffin Theater and Players Riverboat Casino. Superman has had to take up a day job bagging groceries at the Big John supermarket on the east side of town. If you find it hard to believe, check out the guy carrying two sacks in the parking lot. Why do you think they call it a *super*market?

Superman Statue, Superman Square and Market St., Metropolis, IL 62960

(800) 949-5740

Hours: Always visible

Cost: Free

www.metropolisplanet.com/super2.htm

Directions: On the north side of the town square.

Super Museum & Gift Store, 611 Market St., Metropolis, IL 62960

(618) 524-5518

Hours: Daily 9A.M.–5P.M.

Cost: Adults $3, Kids (5 & under) Free

Directions: Adjacent to the town square.

METROPOLIS
Robert Stroud, also known as The Birdman of Alcatraz, was buried in Metropolis' Masonic Cemetery after dying in 1963.

MT. VERNON
On April 14, 1897, Mount Vernon residents spotted a flying man "swimming through the air with an electric light on his back."

MUDDY
The Muddy Post Office (Maple & Public) is currently the nation's second smallest. The USPS planned to close the small hut, but after residents complained, a larger facility was proposed.

Mt. Olive
Mother Jones's Grave

Her name was Mary Harris, but most called her Mother Jones. Mother Jones was a labor organizer who got her start in Chicago after the Great Fire of 1871 when she was already in her forties. She didn't know she had almost 60 good years ahead of her. In 1898, Mother Jones spoke for the rights of miners who were battling with coal companies in Virden, Illinois. Before the strike ended, 10 miners were dead.

Four of those murdered were buried in the Union Miners Cemetery in Mt. Olive. After Mother Jones died at the age of 100 on November 30, 1930, she was laid to rest here, too. A bronze portrait of Mother Jones adorns a large monument that looks far from proletarian.

Union Miners Cemetery, North Lake Ave., Mt. Olive, IL 62069

Hours: Daily 9A.M.–5P.M.

Cost: Free

Directions: North of town on Old Rte. 66 (Lake Ave.).

OBLONG
It is illegal to have sex on your wedding day in Oblong, but only if simultaneously hunting or fishing.

O'FALLON
Actor **William Holden** was born William Franklin Beedle in O'Fallon on April 17, 1918.

TAMAROA
A UFO hovering over Tamaroa on November 14, 1957, caused power outages throughout the area.

TROY
Unexplained crop circles appeared in a field near Troy in 1991 and 1992.

WILLIAMSON COUNTY
Williamson County almost seceded from the Union during the Civil War. The new state intended to call itself Egypt.

Olney
White Squirrel Town

Strange as it sounds, most of the gray squirrels in this small town are albinos . . . and the locals want to keep it that way! The first white squirrels were brought to town in 1902, and there was a population explosion. Olney soon dubbed itself "Home of the White Squirrels." Brown squirrels were rounded up and transported to other communities in an ongoing effort to preserve Olney's albino population.

In some ways, these rodents rule over the folks of Olney, not the other way around. By law, white squirrels have the right-of-way on all local roads. If you run over one, it'll cost you $25, and if you have a cat, you must keep it on a leash when outdoors. The police department's patches have a white squirrel silhouette on them. Who's in charge here?

The number of white squirrels has diminished in recent years. Some blame inbreeding. Others blame human encroachment and interaction. If you're out squirrel-watching, look closely; if the critter you spot doesn't move, it's probably one of the many white squirrel lawn ornaments used to replace the vanishing breed.

City Park, Rte. 130, Olney, IL 62450

(618) 392-2241

Hours: Daily 8 A.M.–10 P.M.

Cost: Free

Directions: All over town, but mainly in City Park.

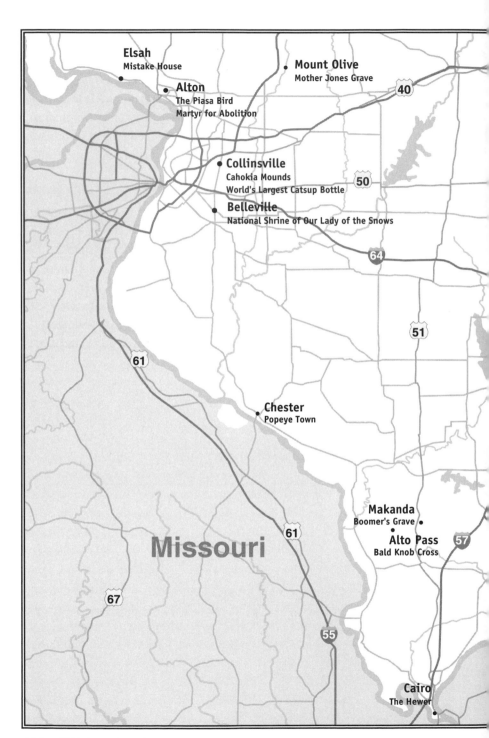

Elsah
Mistake House

Mount Olive
Mother Jones Grave

40

Alton
The Piasa Bird
Martyr for Abolition

Collinsville
Cahokia Mounds
World's Largest Catsup Bottle

50

Belleville
National Shrine of Our Lady of the Snows

64

51

61

Chester
Popeye Town

Makanda
Boomer's Grave

Alto Pass
Bald Knob Cross

57

Missouri

61

67

55

Cairo
The Hewer

Olney
White Squirrel Town

Indiana

Benton
Hard Days Night
Old Franklin Jail Museum

Metropolis
Superman's Hometown

6

THEME TOURS

*O*ddball spots must be experienced to be appreciated—armchair travel is no way to spend your vacation. This book is not intended to be a passive experience. Get up, gas up, and go.

If you plan your trip efficiently, you can visit an oddball spot every half hour or so, making it easy to visit a dozen in a single day. Questions of "Are we there yet?" will be replaced by more engaging dialogue, such as "What the hell is that?" and "Do you think that person is crazy?" Imagine the time you'll have!

And if you're creative, you can map your trip around a theme. That's what this chapter is all about: Theme Tours. The first, the Dead Circus Sideshow Tour, is a statewide trek touching the final resting places of Illinois's strangest deceased citizens. The next two tours, the Mob Mania Tour and the Murder Mania Tour, are listings of Chicago-area crime sites. Pick your favorite crimes, grab a metro-area map, and away you go. An oddball odyssey makes for a perfect Sunday drive!

Dead Circus Sideshow

According to the Illinois Bureau of Tourism, any weekend in this state you're "A Million Miles From Monday™," but oddly enough, you're barely 50 miles from the closest grave of a dead circus sideshow performer, or somebody who might have been. The Fat Man, the Tall Man, the Devil Baby, the Deli-Sliced Duo—they're all here!

Hard to believe? Not really. Illinois has a long sideshow history. Chicago's first public performance was a freak show; in 1834, a "Mr. Bowers" ate burning sealing wax and dropped molten lead on his tongue to the delight of the early settlers. He followed it with a ventriloquist act. Hucksters begged Mrs. O'Leary to be part in a touring sideshow after her cow burned down the city, but she turned them all down, dozens of them. The 1893 Columbian Exposition had the Streets of Cairo where men charmed snakes and Little Egypt danced the Hootchie Kootchie, and the 1933 Century of Progress had a 72-resident Midget Village.

So why shouldn't you join in the fun just because the performers are all dead? Make a weekend of it: the Dead Circus Sideshow Tour! Here's how: Start your journey downstate in Alton, home of . . .

The Gentle Giant.

The World's Tallest (Dead) Man

Harold and Addie Wadlow knew they had a special child. When young Robert entered kindergarten in 1923, he was 5' 6.5" tall and wore the clothes of a 17-year-old. By the fifth grade he was 6' 5" and Harold decided, at long last, to bring his son in for his first checkup. A doctor at Barnes Hospital in St. Louis diagnosed the problem: Robert had an overactive pituitary gland, and there was no known way to correct the problem, at least not at the time.

Wadlow continued to grow. At age 13, he was declared the World's Tallest Boy Scout at 7' 4" and by his 1936 high school graduation he had reached 8' 3.5". He initially resisted the temptation to become a full-time sideshow attraction and enrolled at Shurtleff College, but withdrew after one year. He then signed up for a six-week stint with Ringling Brothers Circus; his "act" consisted of walking out and standing in center ring for a few minutes. He also made a goodwill tour for the International Shoe Company, which provided him with free shoes. The shoes were size 37½ AA.

People everywhere loved him. An Indian tribe in Minnesota "adopted" Wadlow and named him Tall Pine. Folks around Alton dubbed him "The Gentle Giant" for his quiet, humble demeanor. But sometimes his patience was challenged, for children were known to kick him in the shins to see if he was standing on stilts.

Wadlow never stopped growing, and it would lead to his demise. While making an appearance at the Lumberman's Festival in Manistee, Michigan, a misadjusted leg brace rubbed his ankle to the point of infection. At the age of 22, on July 15, 1940, Wadlow died from a fever brought on by that infection. At the time he died, he was 8' 11.1" tall and weighed 491 pounds, a world record!

Thousands of Alton residents turned out for Wadlow's funeral. His 10-foot casket took 12 pall bearers to carry to the Upper Alton Cemetery (2090 Oakwood). To prevent the theft of his body, Wadlow was sealed in a sarcophagus and cement was poured over it. An honor guard from the Order of DeMolay stood over the grave until the cement hardened.

Wadlow has not been forgotten in Alton. Quite the contrary; this town is wacko for Wadlow. In his honor, citizens erected a life-sized bronze statue in a small park across from their history museum. Inside the museum, you can purchase 18.5" footprints cut out of construction paper printed with Robert's statistics, or you can see a pair of his enormous shoes.

Alton Museum of History and Art, Loomis Hall, 2809 College Ave., Alton, IL 62002-6426 (618) 462-2763

Cost: Adults $1, Kids 50¢

Museum Hours: Monday–Friday 10A.M.–4P.M., Saturday–Sunday 1–4P.M.

Statue Hours: Always visible

www.altonweb.com/history/wadlow/

Directions: On Route 140 (College Ave.); Wadlow's statue is across the street.

From Alton, head northeast to Decatur, a watering hole for . . .

Displaced Circus Animals

There's no guarantee the free-roaming circus animals spotted in and around Decatur are dead, but considering the bitter winters, it's a safe bet. Still, keep your car windows rolled up and your picnic basket in the trunk—this town is a genuine Lion Country Safari!

In July 1917, a man picking flowers along the Sangamon River, Thomas Gulliet, was mauled by an adult African lion. Four people riding in a car were jumped by the same cat later in the month. More than 300 Decaturites formed a posse and scoured the countryside, but Nellie the Lion (as named by the press) was never captured. How did she get to Decatur in the first place? Nobody knew.

Another cat, a panther, stuck around a little longer. It was first spotted, and fired upon, on October 25, 1955. It returned a decade later on June 25, 1965, to chase a woman's car. Several days later it stole the sack lunches of three children picnicking in Lincoln Park. In June 1967, the cat was blamed for killing 20 local sheep. It was also spotted tearing up an electric fence near the Macon Seed Company.

And how about crocodiles? Three have been nabbed while swimming in Lake Decatur, one each in 1937, 1966, and 1971. A fourth found its way into town and was captured at 895 W. Eldorado Street in 1967. If you want to see these critters, keep your eyes peeled for residents sporting fancy handbags and boots.

Finally, a kangaroo was sighted by Rosemary Hopwood on July 14, 1975. It was hopping down Route 128. Kangaroos are less dangerous than large felines and crocodiles, but you should never challenge them to a boxing match.

So let this be a warning to those of you traveling with small pets. Pass up Decatur if you plan to walk little Fifi.

Decatur Chamber of Commerce, 100 Merchant St., Decatur, IL 62523

(217) 422-2200

Hours: Always possible

Cost: Free

Directions: All over town.

Next stop? Chicago. The Hog Butcher Capital of the World put its

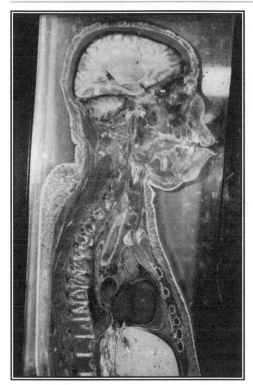

Never play with a food processor!
Photo by author, courtesy of the Museum of Science and Industry, Chicago

cleavers into service to create one of the city's weirdest attractions . . .

The Deli-Sliced Duo

They're gruesome, gray, and gag-inspiring: The Deli-Sliced Duo, or as I prefer to call them, Mr. and Ms. Carver, star attractions at the Museum of Science and Industry. As disturbing as it sounds, somebody once ran two cadavers through a deli slicer set on "Extra Thick," all in the name of science. Who says biology is dull?

The male was cut into inch-thick slabs horizontally, while the female was sliced vertically from head to toe in profile. The cross sections are attractively presented between panes of glass so they can be viewed from either side, a complete set of anatomically correct stained glass windows.

Several of the displays could benefit from a formaldehyde fill-up as the level of the suspending liquid has dropped, but that's a minor complaint. Whatever the Carvers' condition, it's important to appreciate the Museum of Science and Industry's efforts to expose you to what you may never have wanted to see.

Museum of Science and Industry, 5700 S. Lake Shore Dr., Chicago, IL 60637-2093 (773) 684-1414

Hours: Monday–Friday 9:30A.M.–4P.M. (5:30P.M. summers), Saturday–Sunday 9:30A.M.–5:30P.M.

Cost: Adults $7, Seniors(65+) $6, Kids $3.50, Thursdays free

www.msichicago.org

Directions: In Jackson Park off Lake Shore Drive at 57th St. The couple is displayed in the Green Stairwell.

Another Chicago oddity was once a sideshow all by himself but has since been overshadowed by Nobel Peace Prize enthusiasts and other do-gooders.

He's baaaaack . . .

The Devil Baby

Back in 1913, a pious Italian girl married an atheist who cursed the portrait of Jesus she had hung on their wall. "I'd rather have the Devil live here than have that picture hang on our wall!" he screamed, or something like that.

He got his wish. When the baby was born it had cloven feet, scales, horns, and could talk and smoke cigars. Not knowing what to do, the woman brought the baby to Hull House and turned it over to Jane Addams, the living saint of the West Side downtrodden.

Jane cared for the Devil Baby as if it were her own . . . that is, if she would have locked her own child up in the attic for the rest of its natural life! Word got around Chicago that the Devil Baby could be viewed for 25¢. A quarter was a lot of money at the time but well worth it. Addams described in her Hull House memoirs how she turned away dozens of visitors each day. "There's no Devil Baby here," she'd tell the disappointed Satan-seekers.

Likely story. Addams's denials weren't enough to counteract numerous sightings of an adult Devil seen driving around Chicago in a red convertible for years to come, nor the eerie face spotted peering out of Hull House's attic windows at night. Hollywood used the Hull House Devil Baby as the inspiration for *Rosemary's Baby*.

The staff at the Hull-House Museum sometimes bristle when asked about the Devil Baby. They try to focus your attention on Addams's other accomplishments, like her 1931 Nobel Peace Prize for founding the Women's International League for Peace and Freedom, her pivotal role in the creation of the NAACP, or her being the first female to receive an honorary doctorate from Yale. Blah, blah, blah. Just tell us where Satan's Child is, thank you very much!

Jane Addams Hull House, 800 S. Halsted St., Chicago, IL 60607-7017

(312) 413-5353

Hours: Monday–Friday 10A.M.–4P.M., Sunday Noon–5P.M.

Cost: Free

www.uic.edu/jaddams/hull/hull_house.html

Directions: On the east end of the UIC campus, one block south of the Eisenhower Expressway.

Who better to haul around a bunch of dead sideshow performers than a bunch of dead circus roadies? You'll find them in Forest Park at . . .

Showman's Rest

A train carrying the Hagenback-Wallace traveling circus was rammed by a troop train near Ivanhoe, Indiana, on June 22, 1918. Many carnies and performers perished in the resulting blaze, and bodies were difficult to identify. Rather than ship all 86 victims back to their hometowns (which weren't often known), the owners buried 56 in a large plot called Showman's Rest in Forest Park.

Granite elephants guard the dead, their trunks lowered as a sign of respect. Many of the gravestones indicate only the victims' professions or nicknames, such as "Four-Horse Driver" and "Baldy." Also buried here was Edward Kann, the Fat Man, who took up two spots. Today the plot contains other performers who did not die in the crash but still gave their lives to the circus.

Legend has it that you can hear the painful cry of ghost elephants here at night, but none were buried at Woodlawn, nor were any killed in the Ivanhoe wreck. More likely, the trumpeting pachyderms are wafting over from the nearby Brookfield Zoo.

Woodlawn Cemetery, 7600 W. Cermak Rd., Forest Park, IL 60130

(708) 442-8500

Hours: Daily 9A.M.–5P.M.

Cost: Free

Directions: To the west of the main entrance off Cermak Rd.

If you had your heart set on a dead elephant, head west out of the Windy City to Oquawka, where you can say . . .

Good-bye, Norma Jean

. . . Norma Jean the Elephant, that is. This poor creature, star of the Clark and Walters Circus, was chained to the tallest tree on the block on the night of July 17, 1972. Lightning struck, and she was killed instantly.

Norma Jean's handler, unable to move her 6,500-pound carcass, buried her where she dropped. A memorial wall topped with a small bronze elephant marks her final resting place.

Norma Jean Monument, Fifth St. and Mercer, Oquawka, IL 61469

Hours: Always visible

Cost: Free

Directions: Fifth Street between Mercer and Clay.

A man weighing one-sixth of Norma Jean's mass received slightly better funeral arrangements when he was planted in an oversized crate in Mt. Sterling.

The World's Fattest (Dead) Man

Robert Earl Hughes was born in the Illinois town of Fish Hook in 1926, weighing in at 11.5 pounds. As the years rolled on, so did Hughes. On his sixth birthday he tipped the scales at 203. By his early thirties he had maxed out at 1,069 pounds, earning the title of the World's Fattest Man. His upper arms were 40 inches in circumference, his chest was 122 inches, and his waist 124 inches.

Hughes used his weight to earn money at personal appearances, but his girth became a liability when he contracted the measles and could not fit through the door of Indiana's Bremen Hospital. On July 10, 1958, he passed away in his travel van in the hospital parking lot.

His 1,041-pound body was returned to the family plot in Brown County. The burial became its own sideshow when the piano-crate-sized coffin was opened for everyone to get one last gawking look. A few enterprising folk sold souvenir photos. A crane lowered Hughes to his final resting place. His gravestone gives a scant record of the local boy who made it big . . . really, really big.

Benville Cemetery, Mt. Sterling, IL 62353

Hours: 9A.M.–5P.M.

Cost: Free

Directions: At the first fork in the road heading east out of Siloam Springs State Park.

Double-wide grave.

Mob Mania

Ask anyone, *anywhere*, to play a game of word association, and throw out the name Chicago. You'll invariably get a response like "Gangsters!" or "Bang! Bang!" The response is the same, from Valley Girls to Himalayan sherpas. Why else would Europeans propose that EuroDisney's Main Street be fashioned after 1920s Chicago, complete with machine gun-toting mobsters? (Disney's corporate offices killed the idea faster than Capone rubbed out a rat.)

It's not as if Chicago didn't earn its reputation. During the early part of the century there were more than 1,000 gangland hits in Chicago, but only 4 were successfully prosecuted. One intersection in the "Little Hell" neighborhood—Deadman's Corner at Oak and Cleveland—saw 42 unsolved murders between 1910 and 1911. Face it, Chicago and the Mob have received a tommy gun wedding, and nothing the City does will change that.

City Hall has been almost rabid in its anti-Mob tourist policy. For years, Mayor Richard J. Daley blocked the shooting of movies that put Chicago in a bad light in relation to gangsters. Capone's Chicago, a multimedia show narrated by a robotic Scarface, went out of business after being ignored by the City's tourism establishment. And Untouchable Tours gets no mention in City-funded promotional material, either.

It takes a dedicated traveler to find the crime sites that made Chicago world famous. Most buildings associated with Capone have met the wrecking ball. You won't find memorial plaques. You won't see a tommy gun on the City Seal. When it comes to the Mob, you're on your own.

THOUGHTS FROM AL CAPONE

You can get much farther with a smile, a kind word, and a gun than you can with a smile and a kind word.

I've given the public what the public wants. I never had to send out high-pressure salesmen. I could never meet the demand.

They blamed everything but the Chicago Fire on me.

A man's home is his fortress.

Al Capone's Home and Businesses

Al Capone was not a Chicago native. New York Mob boss Little John
Torrio moved Capone to Chicago to "manage" the Four Deuces Brothel.
It was just a few doors down from Colosimo's Cafe, a Mob joint. Capone
was in charge of beating up and torturing snitches in the basement,
known as The Vault. Eventually Torrio would give Capone a controlling
share in the Four Deuces.

Capone had a bungalow built on the South Side where he ended up
living for nine years, from 1922 to 1931. Its commonplace exterior doesn't
hint at its fortresslike amenities, like solid cement walls and steel doors. If,
as his business card claimed, he was a "Second-Hand Furniture Dealer," he
was excessively security conscious.

Al opened an office on two floors of the Metropole Motel, across the
street from the Four Deuces, and kept regular business hours on Sundays.
Capone had a corner office on the fourth floor, and to be on the safe side
his high-backed chair was bulletproof. By 1925, at age 26, he was running
a 1,000-person operation earning $300,000 a week.

The City of Chicago demolished the Metropole just before the 1968 Democratic Convention. Some people tried to get his Prairie Avenue home designated a National Historic Landmark, but the City and Italian American groups put the kibosh on that. The Sons of Italy claimed that naming Capone's home as historic would "assist in the stereotyping and defamation of all Italian Americans," or at least the ones who were not Mob members already.

Al Capone's Home, 7244 S. Prairie, Chicago, IL 60619

Hours: Private residence; view from street

Cost: Free

Directions: Four blocks east of State at 72nd St.

Four Deuces Brothel, 2222 S. Wabash, Chicago, IL 60616

Hours: Demolished; next to Costello Glass and Aluminum

Cost: Free

Directions: One block south of Cermak, one block east of State.

Metropole Motel, 2300 S. Michigan, Chicago, IL 60616

Hours: Demolished in 1975; now a Chevrolet City dealership

Cost: Free

Directions: Two blocks east of State, one block south of Cermak.

Al Capone's Suburban Headquarters

Most city folk reach a point when the rat race starts to get to them, so they move to the suburbs. Al Capone was no exception. When the mayor turned up the heat, the Mob moved to Cicero. Scarface took up residence in the Hawthorne Inn while keeping his place on the South Side. Capone's brother Ralph ran the Cotton Club four blocks away.

The Hawthorne Inn wasn't exactly quieter than the city—Bugs Moran once shot the place up with 1,000 rounds—but at least Al could find parking. Capone controlled the Hawthorne Race Track and bought a controlling interest in the Cicero newspaper, the *Cicero Tribune*, after crusading editor Robert St. John had been calling for the Mob to get out of town. St. John resigned after he learned of his new boss's identity.

But not all was perfect in suburbia. Al's brother Frank was accidentally shot and killed by undercover officers near the Cotton Club. The police were trying to prevent ballot stuffing in Cicero's 1924 election, as if that were even possible.

Capone moved his operations back to Chicago in 1927 after the election of Republican Big Bill Thompson, Chicago's most crooked mayor.

Hawthorne Inn, 4827 W. Cermak Rd., Cicero, IL 60804

Hours: It burned down in 1970

Cost: Free

Directions: One block west of Cicero and Cermak (22nd St.).

Big Jim Hits the Floor

Before there was Al Capone there was Big Jim Colosimo. Big Jim was the Chicago connection for his NYC Mob boss and nephew, Little John Torrio. Colosimo ran his operations out of his South Side drinking establishment, Colosimo's Cafe.

Mob ties aside, it was a wonderful place: a converted warehouse with green velvet wallpaper, clouds and angels flying high overhead, and a hydraulic stage to raise the dancers up where you could see them. But it all went bye-bye when Big Jim hit the floor.

Colosimo was executed on May 11, 1920, in a hit ordered by Little John. Torrio felt Big Jim wasn't spending enough time on the family business, and too much time with his new bride. The hit took place at Colosimo's Cafe; Torrio told Big Jim to wait for a booze shipment, and Frankie Yale (reportedly, though some think it was Al Capone) showed up instead. Big Jim was shot twice, once behind the right ear.

Big Jim was denied a religious burial by the Catholic Church because he had recently dumped his wife, cathouse madam Victoria Moresco, to marry a 19-year-old nightclub singer, Dale Winter.

Colosimo's Cafe, 2126 S. Wabash, Chicago, IL 60616

Hours: Destroyed; now a parking lot

Directions: One block east of State and one block north of Cermak.

Geraldo Goes Digging

Al Capone set up his second Chicago office at the Lexington Hotel where he worked until the day he was indicted on tax charges. Rumor had it the mobster had buried loot in the Lexington's basement, bricked in behind a false wall. Everyone in Chicago knew the rumor, including the Mob, yet Geraldo Rivera thought he'd be the one to crack the mystery.

Geraldo chose to open the vault on a two-hour, live TV special in April 1986. He sang "Chicago," fired a Thompson submachine gun, and detonated sticks of dynamite. After an hour and a half of this painful buildup, a mini-bulldozer crashed through the basement wall. Geraldo rushed in, cameras rolling, only to find a couple of empty bottles. No loot, no skeletons, no aged whiskey. It almost ruined his career.

The City demolished the Lexington in the months leading up to the 1996 Democratic National Convention. The move was reminiscent of the last days of the Metropole. Today, a vacant lot marks the spot. It's not unthinkable that there could still be a stash just below the surface in a hidden basement vault that neither Geraldo nor the City unearthed, but it certainly isn't worth an afternoon digging to find out.

Lexington Hotel, 2135 S. Michigan Ave., Chicago, IL 60616

Hours: Torn down; now a vacant lot

Directions: At the northeast corner of Cermak and Michigan.

Rat-a-tat-tat! Happy Valentine's Day!

St. Valentine's Day Massacre

Al Capone picked a good day in 1929 to gun down seven of Bugs Moran's men. He had hoped to get Bugs, too, but as Daffy Duck learned, that isn't so easy.

Four of Capone's men dressed as policemen raided Moran's liquor warehouse at the SMC Cartage Company on Clark Street. Moran's hoods thought it was a real bust and stood up against the wall as ordered. A thousand rat-a-tat-tats later and five thugs, a dentist, and a mechanic were dead, or almost dead. The only survivor, Frank Gusenberg, claimed, "Nobody shot me," to the first police on the scene, then died from his non-bullet holes. Moran was almost one of the victims, but when he saw the (fake) police cruiser drive up, he headed in the other direction.

At the time all this was happening, Capone was busy making himself overly visible, and therefore incredibly guilty, in Miami. Bugs Moran assessed the situation: "Only Capone kills like that."

The City tore down the garage in 1967, and 417 of the bullet-ridden bricks were sold to a Canadian developer. He had them installed in the men's bathroom of the Banjo Palace karaoke bar in Vancouver. When the place closed, individual bricks were offered for $1,000 each on the Internet. Interest wasn't great and none were sold.

Today, the massacre site is a parking lot. Some claim to hear moans near the murder location. Others say dogs won't go near it, or freak out if they do.

SMC Cartage Company, 2122 N. Clark St., Chicago, IL 60614

Hours: Torn down; now a private parking lot

Directions: One block north of Armitage, just west of Lincoln Park.

Al Capone's Grave and Julia the Uncorruptable

The end for Al Capone was far from glamorous. After being convicted of income tax evasion on October 17, 1931, Capone was sentenced to 11 years in federal prison. He served time in Atlanta, Georgia, and Alcatraz where other mobsters referred to him as "The Wop with the Mop." Capone was released in 1939, partially paralyzed from advanced syphilis, and went off to Miami to die. His final days were spent fishing off his dock and drooling into his bathrobe.

Scarface was originally buried on the South Side at Mount Olivet Cemetery (2755 W. 111th St.), where a monument still stands, but his body was moved to Hillside in 1950 to discourage body snatchers. At his family plot at Mount Carmel, only his headstone has been stolen . . . twice. Scarface's fans often leave offerings at his grave, like coins and cans of beer.

While you're at Mount Carmel, look for the nearby grave of Julia Buccola Petta, a woman who died in childbirth in 1921. Her monument is topped with a bride in a wedding dress and has a picture of Petta in her coffin. If you can't read Italian, the caption says the photo was taken six years *after* her death. Julia was dug up at her mother's request after she had strange dreams of Julia being buried alive. Julia was indeed dead, but she had not rotted at all! Some claim you can smell the scent of roses near her grave, even in the dead of winter, proof of her "uncorruptability."

Mount Carmel Cemetery, 1400 S. Wolf Rd., Hillside, IL 60162

(630) 449-8300

Hours: Daily 9A.M.–5P.M.

Cost: Free

Directions: Turn right from Roosevelt Rd. gate, six markers down on the right, behind shrubs.

OTHER GANGSTERS BURIED IN MOUNT CARMEL

Angelo "Bloody Angelo" Genna Hit man for the Genna bootleg gang. Dion O'Banion's henchmen shotgunned Genna while he was looking to buy a home. He ran into a lamppost on the corner of Ogden and Hudson on May 25, 1925.

Antonio "Tony the Gent" Genna Advisor to the Genna bootleg gang. Tony was shot five times in the back while talking to Guiseppe "The Cavalier" Nerone outside a grocery store.

Mike "The Devil" Genna Hit man for the Genna bootleg gang. The Devil was shot on Western Avenue by police during a high-speed chase. He died after kicking the ambulance attendant who was trying to stop the bleeding from Genna's femoral artery.

Jake Lingle Corrupt *Chicago Tribune* reporter. Lingle was executed near the Randolph Street Station (in the pedway beneath Michigan Ave.).

"Machine Gun" Jack McGurn Coordinator of the Valentine's Day Massacre for Al Capone. McGurn was killed on Valentine's Day in 1936 as payback. It happened at the Avenue Recreation Rooms (805 N. Milwaukee). A valentine card was left on his chest that read, "You've lost your job/You've lost your dough/Your jewels and handsome houses/But things could be worse, you know/You haven't lost your trousers."

Frank Nitti Replaced Capone as head of the Chicago Mob. Nitti shot himself on the railroad tracks near Harlem and Cermak on March 19, 1943.

Dion "Deany" O'Banion Rival of Capone's. Deany was gunned down on November 10, 1924, in his Schofield's Flower Shop (738 N. State) across the street from Chicago's Holy Name Cathedral.

Earl "Hymie" Weiss Tried to kill Al Capone three times. Hymie was shot on the steps of Holy Name Cathedral (735 N. State) on October 11, 1926. There's still a bullet hole in the cornerstone.

Beware the Lady in Orange.

John Dillinger Death Site

Public Enemy #1 finally bought the farm on July 22, 1934, after sitting through the movie *Manhattan Melodrama* with Polly Hamilton, his girlfriend, and her friend Anna Sage. Dillinger had recently undergone plastic surgery and was living with Hamilton under the alias of Jimmy Lawrence at 2420 N. Halsted Street. Hamilton later claimed she thought he worked at the Chicago Board of Trade.

Sage, a brothel madam and Romanian immigrant who feared deportation, ratted on Dillinger to Melvin Purvis's FBI team as a way to curry favor with the feds. (It didn't work; they deported her after Dillinger was dead.) She informed the team that her trio would be at the Biograph that night; when they exited, 16 agents moved in. Dillinger made a run for the alley to the south. Three bullets hit Dillinger in the back, head, and side, killing him immediately. Two moviegoers were also shot, though neither seriously.

Rumors circulated that a woman dressed in red had fingered Dillinger. However, Sage was wearing an orange skirt and Hamilton had a tan ensemble. Nevertheless, the story of the Woman in Red continues.

Crowds flocked to dab some of Dillinger's blood off the street. A helpful bystander mixed soda water from a nearby bar with the blood to make it go further for the handkerchief-toting ghouls. For weeks, many more bloodied handkerchiefs were sold around Chicago than could have ever been dipped in the blood.

Dillinger's body was placed on public view at the Cook County Morgue; 15,000 filed past his body. A photo taken that night was the origin of the 14-inch (20-inch erect) penis rumor. Rigor mortis had caused his arm, not his penis, to push up the sheet around his groin. Some news photographs were altered for modesty's sake.

WAS THAT REALLY DILLINGER?

Conspiracy theorists believe that Dillinger was not gunned down outside the Biograph and that the victim was really small-time Wisconsin thug Jimmy Lawrence. Consider that Dillinger's autopsy wasn't released until 30 years after his death, perhaps for good reason:

➡ The body at the morgue was shorter and heavier than Dillinger's body.

➡ The body at the morgue had brown eyes, but Dillinger's were blue.

➡ The body's heart showed damage from rheumatic fever, though Dillinger never had the disease.

➡ Two of Dillinger's telltale scars had mysteriously vanished from his body.

The real Jimmy Lawrence disappeared, coincidentally, the day of Dillinger's shooting. Could Anna Sage have arranged a date with Lawrence to give Dillinger an out? J. Edgar Hoover or his agents might have been too embarrassed to admit they had made a terrible mistake, so they perpetrated an elaborate hoax.

So where did Dillinger end up, if in fact he survived? The most popular story says he married and moved to Oregon where he died or disappeared sometime during the 1940s.

Several students from a "college of embalming" stopped by to make a death mask, but FBI agents confiscated the cast when they realized the group had no credentials. Dillinger's brain was removed and reportedly sent to Northwestern University for study. From there it ended up on a shelf in Kearney, Nebraska, or in the hands of Jimmy Hoffa, depending on whom you believe. His brain was definitely missing before Dillinger's body arrived in Indiana. The family threatened to sue the FBI, but it assured them it had been put to good use in a "scientific study."

The Biograph's exterior looks much like it did when Dillinger was shot. Occasionally, on July 22, the Biograph replays *Manhattan Melodrama* for the Dillinger-era price of 25¢. After the show, follow his final steps into the alley just south of the entrance, today known as "Dillinger's Alley." Some have claimed to see his ghost on the anniversary of his death.

Biograph Theater, 2433 N. Lincoln Ave., Chicago, IL 60614

(773) 348-4123

Hours: Always visible

Cost: Free

www.geocities.com/Athens/Olympus/4172/

Directions: One block north of Fullerton Ave.

Baby Face Nelson's Final Shootout, Death Site, and Grave

George "Baby Face" Nelson became Public Enemy #1 after his former gangmate Dillinger was killed outside the Biograph Theater. His ranking on the FBI list didn't last very long. Nelson, his wife Helen, and fellow criminal John Paul Chase were ambushed by agents near Lake Geneva, Wisconsin, on November 27, 1934. They escaped and were chased into Illinois, exchanging gunfire with police as they fled toward Chicago at high speeds.

Near Barrington, Nelson's fuel pump was shot out, and he turned his car into the entrance to what is now Langendorf Park. The G-men skidded past the road, stopped, hopped out of their car, and were promptly gunned down by the gangsters. FBI agents Herman Hollis (an agent who had shot John Dillinger four months earlier) and Samuel Cowley were killed, but not before pumping 17 rounds into Nelson. Chase loaded Nelson's body into the FBI car and escaped with Nelson's wife.

A stone monument to the two slain FBI agents, and another who Nelson had killed in Koerner's Corners, Wisconsin, the previous April, stands near the site of the shootout.

Langendorf Park, Route 14, Barrington, IL 60010

(847) 381-0687

Hours: Always visible

Cost: Free

Directions: Rte. 14 and Bryant, three blocks east of Rte. 59.

Nelson was likely killed in Barrington, but his body didn't turn up until the following day, miles away near a cemetery in Skokie. His nude body was wrapped in a blanket and dumped in a ditch adjoining St. Paul's Cemetery. Helen Gillis and John Paul Chase abandoned the FBI car in Winnetka, then fled in opposite directions.

St. Paul's Cemetery, 5400 W. Conrad St., Skokie, IL 60077

Hours: Always visible

Cost: Free

Directions: Adjacent to St. Paul's Cemetery, on the southwest corner of Conrad St. and Long Ave., three blocks south of Dempster, one block west of Gross Point Rd.

St. Paul's felt no special obligation to bury Nelson just because he was dumped there. Nelson was instead buried in St. Joseph's Cemetery in River Grove under his birth name, Lester Gillis. Helen Gillis was apprehended in Michigan, and Chase was picked up in California.

St. Joseph's Cemetery, 3100 N. Thatcher, River Grove, IL 60171

(708) 453-0184

Hours: Daily 9A.M.–5P.M.

Cost: Free

Directions: At the intersection of Cumberland/Thatcher and Belmont.

Untouchable Tours

If you want to see Mob sites but are not good with maps, and not self-conscious about riding around in a black bus filled with bullet holes, Untouchable Tours will do the work for you. Far from an academic, stuffy, guided tour, Untouchables is a two-hour, nonstop show, complete with sing-alongs, fake gunfire, raffles, and a few surprises.

Before departing, you're advised to behave by the costumed driver and tour guide, and since they're the ones with the fake guns, you listen. The bus rolls along past 17 different sites where the thugs relay all the gory details, interspersed with vaudeville banter. Between sights you're treated to Italian opera, card tricks, a "reenactment" of the Great Chicago Fire, and given pointers on dodging bullets.

"Southside" Alton Craig has been running the tours for 10 years, and interest shows no sign of waning. It's the perfect afternoon diversion for out-of-towners and is even appreciated by those not on the tour; you'll see bystanders on the sidewalk getting into the act by laughing, pointing, and machine-gunning the bus through participatory mime. It's all part of the fun, and let's face it, gangsters are F-U-N!

PO Box 43185, Chicago, IL 60643

(773) 881-1195

Hours: Call ahead for reservations

Cost: Adults $22, Kids $16, Switchblade combs $2

Directions: Bus departs from Ohio and Clark Sts.

Get on the bus . . . or else!

Jack Ruby's Grave

Long before he became an assassin's assassin, Jack Ruby was a small-time hustler in Chicago. He changed his name from Jack Rubenstein to "fit in" better with Capone's crowd. Ruby's primary activity was to run numbers for the South Side Mob.

Ruby went on to, if not greater, perhaps more notorious endeavors. Millions watched him kill Lee Harvey Oswald on live TV, supposedly to spare Jackie Kennedy the agony of recounting her husband's murder. He died of cancer while awaiting execution, cancer that Oliver Stone–types think was induced to ensure his silence.

Well, silent he is, six feet under in his old hometown.

Westlawn Cemetery, 7801 W. Montrose Ave., Chicago, IL 60634

(773) 625-8600

Hours: Daily 9A.M.–5P.M.

Cost: Free

Directions: Six blocks west of Harlem.

Chester Gould–Dick Tracy Museum

One interesting response to Chicago's gangland problems was the creation of "Dick Tracy," which debuted on October 4, 1931. Chester Gould's square-jawed crime fighter was the cartoonist's 61st proposal for the *Chicago Tribune*, and the first idea they bought from him.

Events in the strip were loosely based upon events in Chicago. The character "Big Boy" was Al Capone. Each day, readers would follow Tracy as he battled the evil members in the Rogue's Gallery. Dick Tracy fans like to point to the future-thinking Gould and his prediction of a Two-Way Wrist Radio, but they seldom mention his as-yet-unrealized Magnetic Space Coup, Atomic Light, and Floating TV Camera. The comic strip also introduced CrimeStoppers in 1949, years before McGruff. Junior would give weekly crime-fighting tips to young readers, who could then cut the panel out for a notebook.

Gould did most of his strips from his Woodstock home and studio. On the grounds of his home was a miniature Rogue's Gallery "cemetery" for all the villains he had inked out. Gould was buried in Woodstock's Oakland Cemetery after he died on May 11, 1985.

The Chester Gould–Dick Tracy Museum has an impressive collection of Tracy material, like the space-age toy Copmobile, comic strip sketches, and Gould's drawing board. They've also got a gift shop where you can pick up a yellow fedora.

Each year, on the last weekend in June, Woodstock hosts Dick Tracy Days, complete with bands, a parade, a look-alike contest, and the march of the Rogue's Gallery around the town square. At one time they had a shootout play, but somebody complained that their car had been damaged and further performances were halted.

101 N. Johnson St., PO Box 44, Woodstock, IL 60098

(815) 338-8281

Hours: February–December, Thursday–Saturday 11A.M.–5P.M., Sunday 1–5P.M.; January, Saturdays 11A.M.–5P.M.

Cost: Free

user.mc.net/~kfarver/dt/museum.htm

Directions: On the west side of the town square.

American Police Center and Museum

The American Police Center and Museum was opened in 1974 with several goals in mind: to honor fallen and injured police officers, to combat "misinformation" surrounding the events at the 1968 Democratic National Convention, to educate schoolchildren about the dangers of drug use and/or a life of crime, and to act as a repository for Chicago police-obilia.

The Chicago police had what could diplomatically be called an "image problem" following the 1968 riots. Mayor Richard J. Daley made a classic Freudian slip when he claimed, "The policeman isn't there to create disorder. He is there to preserve disorder." According to the Walker Commission, they did just that. But you won't see the Monday-morning quarterback's report at this museum, only the perspective of the events through the eyes of a policeman, shown in a collage of photos. One picture shows a hairy, nude hippie sitting in Lincoln Park while a disinterested, 50-something woman holding a Chihuahua stands behind him. The caption reads "Some demonstrators 'Doing Their Thing.'" Sure, she should have had the dog on a leash, but how much harm could the little Chihuahua do?

The drug exhibit is only slightly less heavy-handed. A black coffin is filled with examples of every street drug imaginable, neatly labeled. You'll see unfamiliar drugs, like Talwin and Cylert, but they've also got Ritalin and Lomotil. Are those street drugs? Will a hyperactive child or a tourist with the trots think they're junkies when they see this?

But if you really want to be beat over the head about the horror of a life of crime, check out the display case labeled "This exhibit may be upsetting to small children and sensitive persons." You'll see dozens of blood-splattered crime and accident scenes lumped together in no particular order, except to shock. The greatest shocks, however, come from two electric chairs in their collection. One invites you to "Feel the effect of sitting in an 'Electric Chair,'" without the voltage, of course. Sorry, no photos allowed! The other electric chair, dubbed The Texas Thunderbolt, came from the Huntsville State Penitentiary. It was first used on February 8, 1924, where "Warden William Miller personally pulled [the switch] to execute 5 over a 2-hour period." Imagine the electric bill!

And would a Chicago police museum be complete without some mention of the Mob or infamous gangsters? They've got the Biograph Theater seat where John Dillinger watched his last movie, the wooden gun he used to escape from an Indiana jail, a copy of Dillinger's Death Mask, Bonnie Parker's Colt 45, and piles of Al Capone junk.

1717 S. State St., Chicago, IL 60616

(312) 431-0005

Hours: Monday–Friday 9:30A.M.–4:30P.M.

Cost: Adults $4, Seniors $3, Kids(3–11) $2.50, Police Officers $1.50

Directions: Five blocks south of Roosevelt on State St.

CHICAGO LAWS

Chicago police are sworn to uphold the law, so don't be caught engaging in any of the following illegal activities:

➡ Wearing pince-nez glasses while driving a car.
➡ Bringing a French poodle to an opera house.
➡ Walking a hog through the city streets without a ring in its nose.
➡ Fishing off the breakwater in your pajamas.
➡ Eating in a burning restaurant.
➡ Installing a pay toilet.
➡ Going outside if you've been deformed, diseased, or maimed so that you are "an unsightly or disgusting object."

Murder Mania
Murder Castle

It is in a strange way reassuring that mass murder is not a modern phenomenon. The case of Herman Mudgett, also known as Dr. H. H. Holmes, is an excellent case in point.

Mudgett built a three-story edifice across the street from his Chicago drugstore in 1892, just prior to the 1893 Columbian Exposition. Locals called it The Castle. By continually hiring and firing construction workers, he was able to keep his blueprints secret. The 60-room building contained a soundproof dungeon, trapdoors, hidden staircases, false walls, a third-floor door that dropped to the alley, sealed rooms that could be locked from the outside and gassed from the inside, and more than one slippery body chute.

The Columbian Exposition and the Lonelyhearts papers provided Mudgett with plenty of victims. The smooth-talking murderer would convince visitors to sign over their savings accounts and insurance policies, and these people who would then "disappear." They would then "reappear" as skeletons, which Mudgett fenced to medical schools, no questions asked. High estimates put the number of victims at 200.

This continued until Mudgett was arrested for bumping off his assistant, Benjamin Pitezel, and his three children in a fraud scam that started in Philadelphia. Word of Mudgett's arrest got back to Chicago, and police entered The Castle. Though no corpses were found, evidence of his sinister operation was damning. Mudgett was executed in Pennsylvania, and his corpse was sealed in cement before burial. Bad as he was, there is no truth to the legend that a lightning bolt struck Mudgett in the neck just as the gallows' trapdoor opened.

The Castle became a tourist attraction (Can you imagine?!!) during the murder trial; people gladly paid 25¢ to see Mudgett's handiwork. But locals thought the place was bad for business, and somebody burned it to the ground on August 19, 1896.

So the next time you hear someone lament, "What is this world coming to?" point out that it could be worse, and was.

701 W. 63rd St., Chicago, IL 60637

Hours: Torn down

Cost: Free

Directions: At 63rd St. and Wallace, where the U.S. Post Office stands today.

Leopold and Loeb

The case of Leopold and Loeb is probably one of the worst examples of what bored, nasty, rich kids can do if they set their minds to it. Nathan Leopold and Richard Loeb were fascinated by crime, so much so they decided to commit the "perfect murder." And because they had convinced one another they were geniuses, they never expected to get caught.

The pair nabbed 13-year-old Bobbie Franks on May 21, 1924, near 49th and Ellis Ave. while he walked home from Kenwood's Harvard Preparatory School. Franks was one of Loeb's distant cousins, so he willingly got into their rented car. Loeb killed the boy with a chisel and the pair dumped his body in a culvert, mutilated with acid, near the Penn Central tracks at 118th Street. They then sent a typed ransom letter to Franks's parents.

All Hyde Park was abuzz with police activity. Loeb even "assisted" the police during the early stages of the investigation before he became a suspect, volunteering, "If I were going to pick out a boy to kidnap or murder, that's just the kind of cocky little son-of-a-bitch I would pick." Smart move, genius boy!

Police found Franks's body, along with Leopold's distinctive eyeglasses. He had dropped them while trying to dispose of the body—Oops! The cops then fished Leopold's Underwood typewriter out of Jackson Park Harbor. It matched the keystrokes on the ransom note. The perfect murder was starting to look far from perfect.

Clarence Darrow, as defense attorney, got the pair to confess to the crime in a plea bargain on July 19, 1924. He then argued that the pair's slave/king sexual relationship put them into a category of psychopaths unable to understand the consequences of their actions. Regardless if this makes any sense, they ended up with life plus 99 years instead of the electric chair, which is what they wanted.

Loeb was stabbed in a shower melee in the Joliet State Prison in 1936. Leopold was paroled in 1958 and moved to Puerto Rico. He worked at the Church of the Brethren Hospital where kids called him Mr. Lollipop until his death in 1971. The pair's crime was the basis for Alfred Hitchcock's *Rope* and the movie *Swoon*.

Leopold's Home, 4754 Greenwood Ave., Chicago, IL 60615

Hours: Demolished; new house on site

Loeb's Home, 5017 S. Ellis Ave., Chicago, IL 60615

Hours: Demolished; new house on site

Franks's Home, 5052 S. Ellis Ave., Chicago, IL 60615

Hours: Demolished; new house on site

Richard Speck's Rampage

Though Richard Speck was not Chicago's first mass murderer, nor its most prolific, he psychologically scarred the city like nobody else. Perhaps it was timing. His brutal murders seemed to usher in an era of ever-increasing violence. A tattoo on his arm read, "Born to Raise Hell," and it was right.

On the night of July 13–14, 1966, Speck talked his way into an apartment rented by student nurses from nearby South Side Community Hospital. Over the next several hours he systematically raped, strangled, and stabbed eight women. A ninth nurse, Corazon Amurao, survived by hiding under a bed.

Based upon Amurao's description, police began looking for a suspect with bad skin and the tattoo on his arm. Speck was hiding out at the Raleigh Hotel (650 N. Dearborn), a North Side flophouse from which he was soon kicked out for bad behavior. Speck attempted suicide by slashing his wrists and ended up at Cook County Hospital. A doctor saw the tattoo and Speck was arrested.

Amurao bravely identified Speck during the trial, resulting in eight death sentences. The executions were later overturned as unconstitutional, and the sentence was changed to 600 years behind bars. In Joliet's Stateville Prison, he painted disturbing pictures of Bambi, and he sold them to outsiders for cigarette money. Speck died of a heart attack on December 5, 1991, but that wasn't the end of the story.

Years after his death, a disturbing jailhouse videotape made in 1988 surfaced. It showed Speck with hormone-created breasts having sex and taking drugs in his cell with fellow inmates. The tape was played nightly, to the horror of Chicago viewers. On the tapes, Speck claimed, "If they only knew how much fun I was having, they would turn me loose." Well, that might be going a bit far.

Speck Murder Site

2319 E. 100th St., Chicago, IL 60617

Hours: Private residence; view from street

Cost: Free

Directions: Six blocks west of Torrence on 100th.

Black Panther Shoot-out

The killing of Black Panther leaders Fred Hampton and Mark Clark on December 4, 1969, was more of a shoot-at than a shoot-out. The Chicago Police, with backing from the FBI, fired 90+ shots to the Panthers' one. Why didn't Hampton fight back? It might have been because it was 4:30A.M. and he was sound asleep, possibly knocked out with secobarbitol-laced Kool-Aid courtesy of infiltrator William O'Neill.

The 21-year-old Hampton had been getting a lot of positive attention in the preceding year. In addition to heading the Illinois Chapter of the Black Panther Party, he had established a Breakfast for Children program, brokered truces between street gangs, and organized a free health clinic for the poor. Talk about a troublemaker!

During an investigation of the incident, Hampton's girlfriend reported that police went into his bedroom while others were cuffing her, fired a shot, and remarked, "There, now he's good and dead." The families of Hampton and Mark Clark received $1.85 million in damages.

"Security Chief" O'Neill acted as one of Hampton's pallbearers. Not until 1973 was the role he played revealed, and of how he was paid a $300 bonus after Hampton's death. This loose cannon also offered the FBI plans for an electric chair to "interrogate" informants and suggested blowing up City Hall with a rocket. To the police's credit, they didn't pay him for either of those ideas. In 1990, O'Neill killed himself by running out onto the Eisenhower Expressway.

2337 W. Monroe Ave., Chicago, IL 60612

Hours: A new home has been built on the site

Cost: Free

Directions: One block east of Western, four blocks north of I-290.

POINT OF CLARIFICATION . . .
Seventeen white Chicago aldermen asked that their names be removed from a resolution honoring **Fred Hampton**, the slain Black Panther leader. They claimed they thought they'd voted for a resolution for Dan Hampton of the Chicago Bears.

John Wayne Gacy's Home

One of the most shocking aspects of the John Wayne Gacy case was the appalling lack of curiosity on the part of everyone involved. Why didn't neighbors wonder about the smell of rotting flesh emanating from his crawlspace? Why didn't the police catch his prior criminal history in Iowa when he was picked up for criminal sexual assault in Illinois? Why wasn't Gacy's wife more suspicious when she found several wallets of young men in her husband's car and dresser? Why couldn't police connect the dots when several of Gacy's teenage workers disappeared, one of whom signed over the title to his car to Gacy, *in Gacy's handwriting*? And why didn't the Secret Service pick up on his arrest record when he was cleared to have a meeting with Rosalynn Carter?

Gacy found many of his victims through his construction business, PDM, which stood for Painting, Decorating, and Maintenance, though more were nabbed at random. His early victims ended up in his crawlspace and in the floor of the garage. Five of his later victims were thrown in the Des Plaines River after the crawlspace was full. The final victim, Robert Piest, was tossed from the Des Plaines River bridge just south of Joliet and was found near the confluence of the Des Plaines and Illinois near Morris.

Though Gacy did make a confession when the police first questioned him—he even drew a map showing where the bodies were hidden—he later recanted the story, saying it had been dragged out of him under duress. Gacy continued to profess his innocence, though he never fully explained how the 27 corpses could have gotten under his house without his knowledge. Gacy's home was eventually demolished. Property values in the neighborhood were (understandably) a concern, and the place had been severely damaged during the excavation of the crawlspace. Today a new home stands on the lot; it's the only modern building on the block.

Gacy spent his Death Row days at the Menard Corrections Center. During his incarceration, he spent time coming up with even more preposterous explanations as to how those bodies ended up under his house and painting Pogo the Clown pictures for mail-order art lovers. He was executed by lethal injection in 1994, but not before he had a chance to announce his engagement to a Centralia woman. Said the lucky lady of her fiancé's notoriety, "I don't believe hardly any of it." His final meal was fried chicken and strawberries.

It is believed that Gacy's ashes were buried in an unmarked grave at Mary Hill Cemetery in Niles, near the graves of his parents John and Marion.

8213 W. Summerdale Ave., Norwood Park, IL 60631

Hours: Private property; view from the street

Cost: Free

Directions: Two blocks east of Cumberland, four blocks south of I-90.

SUBURBAN SLAUGHTERHOUSE

If there's a mantra repeated by suburban Chicago residents, it has to be "I'm sure glad we don't live in that crime-ridden cesspool," referring, of course, to Chicago. It should at least be stated for the record that the region's four most recent killing sprees occurred in the suburbs, not Chicago: John Wayne Gacy in Norwood Park, the Tylenol tampering murders, Laurie Dann's rampage in Winnetka, and Palatine's Brown's Chicken murders.

➡ Victims of the **Tylenol Tamperer** started dropping on September 29, 1982, eventually claiming seven throughout Lombard, Winfield, Schaumburg, and Arlington Heights. The killer was never apprehended.

➡ **Laurie Dann** was a ticking time bomb in the northern suburbs for years. She harassed ex-babysitting clients and mailed arsenic-laced Rice Krispies Squares to strangers. On May 20, 1988, she dumped an ineffectual bomb at Highland Park's Ravinia Elementary School before heading to Winnetka's Hubbard Woods Elementary. There she shot six, killing one child. She ended up breaking into a nearby home where she shot another victim before committing suicide.

➡ And where, on January 8, 1993, were seven **Brown's Chicken** employees murdered in cold blood and stacked like cordwood in the freezer? Not Chicago. Palatine. Police wasted time focusing on a disgruntled ex-employee, but as anyone who has every worked at a fast-food joint knows, *every* former employee is disgruntled. Leads dried up and so did the investigation. The case remains one of Illinois's most notorious unsolved suburban mysteries.

O.J. Spends the Night

Courthouse groupies at the Trail of the Century know the street names of Rockingham and Bundy, but do they know Cumberland? It was here, at the O'Hare Plaza Hotel (now the Wyndham Garden) that O.J. slept on the night of the double murder in Brentwood. Simpson came to Chicago on a business trip and that is where, according to him, he first learned of his ex-wife's death. At the news, he claimed he smashed a drinking glass and cut his hand.

Police had a hard time buying the story, so they began searching the vacant lot adjacent to the hotel, hoping to find the missing murder weapon or the assailant's bloody clothing. They found neither. Since the real killer, or killers, of Ron Goldman and Nicole Brown Simpson is/are still at large, the case is still open. Just ask O.J. The vacant lot's still there. Maybe you can conduct your own investigation.

Wyndham Garden Hotel, Room 915, 5615 N. Cumberland Ave., Chicago, IL 60631

(773) 693-5800

Hours: Year round; call for reservations

Cost: Rooms start at $159/night

Directions: Just south of the Kennedy Expressway at the Cumberland Exit, east of O'Hare.

EPiLOGUE

As you can imagine, many forces work against the survival of roadside oddities: pissed-off neighbors, competing attractions, culture-Nazis, Mother Nature, the Grim Reaper, and simple, basic economics.

Some sites were always fleeting blips on the tourism radar, destined for destruction before they were even opened. Most of Chicago's 1893 Columbian Exposition buildings were built of plaster. They included the Panorama of Kilauea, an erupting Hawaiian volcano with simulated lava; an electrified Egyptian Temple; a Mammoth Crystal Cave; the world's first Ferris wheel; and a lagoon filled with Venetian gondolas, Viking war ships, and a replica of Columbus's *Santa Maria*. The plaster lasted long enough to burn up in a mysteriously convenient conflagration on January 8, 1894, at the end of the Expo.

The 1933 Century of Progress was equally fleeting. Madame Tussaud animated her Torture Chamber so visitors could witness people being stretched, roasted, and hacked to pieces. P. T. Barnum's American Museum recreated Barnum, Tom Thumb, the Fat Lady, and the original Siamese Twins with freakish robots. The 23-story Sky Ride took you up to see the skyline in an RV-sized rocket belching simulated exhaust! But it's all gone, gone to make way for Meigs Field, a dinky airport that services literally dozens of airplanes a day. What a waste.

Many roadside attractions survive only on the health and good fortune of their proprietors. Norvina Thatch built a Whirligig Garden in Future City, just north of Cairo, but it was bulldozed shortly after Thatch died. Similar was the fate of Aldo Piacenza's Birdhouse Garden in Highwood, but instead of bulldozers his elaborate creations were cleared by folk art dealers and collectors.

Other places just go out of business. You used to be able to take a gondola ride on the Des Plaines River after enjoying a dinner at Wheeling's Villa Venice. No more. Do you like airline food but can't stand flying? If Chicago's Ski-Hi Drive-In were still open, you'd be able to dine in the fuselage of an airliner atop its roof. The Midget's Club on Chicago's South Side once catered to the little person's needs. No Dwarf Tossing or Midget Bowling, just proportional barstools, chairs, and tables. But that's gone, too.

Still others have packed up and left town. The Bicycle Museum once housed in Chicago's North Pier moved to Ohio. The 1,500-piece holy relic collection at Peoria's St. Francis Monastery closed when its clerical order relocated to Indiana. Did the Galena Wax Museum's 50-odd Civil War figures end up as candles in the town's knickknack shops after the museum shut its doors? Perhaps. And who even knows what happened to Evanston's Museum of Funeral Service Artifacts, the life-sized Bigfoot replica on display at a resort in Oilfield, or the World's Largest Black Velvet Elvis that once hung in Chicago's World Tattoo Gallery?

Do you get the picture? Fill up your gas tank and hit the road TODAY, before the evil forces to "good taste" drive the offbeat wonders from the landscape.

ACKNOWLEDGMENTS

This book would not have been possible without the assistance, patience, and good humor of many individuals. My thanks go out to the following people for allowing me to interview them about their roadside attractions: Mrs. LaRae Ackerson (Rest Cottage), Carrie Brantley (Egyptian Theater), Jim & Daryl Chady and C. J. & Dorothy Schultz (Hard Day's Nite B&B), George & Winnie Colin (Colin Folk Art), Suzan Cook (Carlock Cemeteries), Alton Craig (Untouchable Tours), Phyllis Danner (John Philip Sousa Library), David Douglass (Dave's Down to Earth Rock Shop), Sandy & Mike Dunphy (The Barn B&B), Ted Frankel (Uncle Fun), Jan Gallimore (Lake County Museum), Mike Gassmann (World's Largest Catsup Bottle), Deborah Gust (Curt Teich Post Card Archives), Margery Hinrichs (Ida Public Library), Richard Jenkins (Lincoln-Douglas Valentine Museum), Callie McKenna (Evergreen Memorial Cemetery), Cookie Oppedisano (Hala Kahiki), Robert Rea (Old Franklin County Jail Museum), Judy Robins and Patrick Sim (The Wood Library–Museum of Anesthesiology), Richard Sklenar (Theatre Historical Society of America), Dr. Charles Smith (African American Heritage Cultural Center & Black Veterans Archives), the staff at Spinach Can Collectibles (Popeye Town), Ed Stockey (Midwest Carver's Museum), Beth Vargo (Chester Gould–Dick Tracy Museum), Jim Warfield (Raven's Grin Inn), Mary Ann Warmack (Alton Museum of History and Art), Melva Wilzbach (Salem Days Fest), and Mimi Witschy (Blue Frog Bar and Grill).

For research assistance, I am indebted to the librarians in the Illinois communities of Belvidere, East Dubuque, Highwood, Lincolnshire, Newton, Mt. Sterling, Sparta, and White Hall. Ken Little was kind enough to review my Chicago Fire material, and I would not have found him without the help of Chris Greve. Also, John Cieciel and the mysterious Tony Shaia have pointed me in the direction of more than a few interesting and out-of-the-way sites.

Friends, family members, and complete strangers willingly volunteered to act as models for the photographs in this book, oftentimes against their better judgment: Jenny Birmingham, John Birmingham, T. J. Birmingham, Brian Conway, "Southside" Alton Craig, Tirza Ernst, Tony Fernandez, Ted Frankel, James Frost, Olga Granat, Tom Granat, Kyle Granat, Taylor Granat, Stephanie Herbek, Ann Grusdis, Eugene Marceron, Mike Musick, Pat O'Brien, Joe Pohlen, Pam Pohlen, Joe T. Pohlen, Zachary Pohlen, Samantha Pohlen, Michael "Shifty" Rubin, Mary Ann Schultz, Tess Shea, Karen Soll, Ed Stockey, Lorraine Swanson, Jim Warfield, and John Wiener. Jim Pohlen, Teresa Pohlen, Matthew Pohlen, Eric Pohlen, and Daniel Pohlen would have gladly confronted the Devil Baby of Hull House had they not been buried by the New Year's Blizzard of 1999. On my travels, I appreciated the hospitality of Curt & Amy Himstedt and Dave Michalak & Elizabeth Wangler.

Without the early support I received for my "zine" *Cool Spots, Oddball Illinois* would not have been written. Steven Svymberky, Patience Allen, Lee Azus, Mark Maynard, Chuck Shepherd, Lorraine Swanson, Liz Clayton, and R. Seth Friedman gave me that encouragement.

Finally, I wish to thank Robert Johnson, Gordon Wells, Bonnie Papke, Kathy Royer, and my ever-understading parents, Joseph and Barbara Pohlen.

RECOMMENDED SOURCES

If you'd like to learn more about the places and individuals in this book, the following are excellent sources.

Introduction
General Illinois Guides
Chicago on Foot, Fifth Edition by Ira J. Bach and Susan Wolfson (Chicago: Chicago Review Press, 1994)

Awesome Almanac—Illinois by Jean F. Blashfield (Fontana, Wisc. B&B Publishing, Inc., 1993)

Daytrip Illinois by Lee N. Godley and Patricia M. O'Rourke (Fulton, Mo. Aphelion Publishing Company, 1997)

Illinois Historical Tour Guide by D. Ray Wilson (Carpentersville, Ill. Crossroads Communications, 1991)

1. Chicago! Chicago!
General Chicago Guides
Metro Chicago Almanac by Don Hayner and Tom McNamee (Chicago: Chicago Sun-Times, 1993)

Hands-On Chicago by Kenan Heise and Mark Frazel (Chicago: Bonus Books, Inc., 1987)

Greater Chicago Historical Tour Guide by D. Ray Wilson (Carpentersville, Ill.: Crossroads Communications, 1989)

Chicago Architecture
Chicago's Famous Buildings by Franz Schulze and Kevin Harrington (Chicago: University of Chicago Press, 1993)

Pocket Guide to Chicago Architecture by Judith Paine McBrien (New York: W. W. Norton, 1997)

The Union Stockyards
The Jungle by Upton Sinclair (New York: New American Library, 1905)

The Chicago Historical Society
What George Wore and Sally Didn't by Rosemary K. Adams (Chicago: Chicago Historical Society, 1998)

The Field Museum
The Man-Eating Lions of Tsavo by J. H. Patterson (Chicago: Field Museum of Natural History, 1925)

The Playboy Mansion
Inside the Playboy Mansion by Gretchen Edgren (Santa Monica, Calif.: General Publishing Group, 1998)

Chicago and Hollywood
Hollywood on Lake Michigan by Arnie Berenstein (Chicago: Lake Claremont Press, 1998)

Bob Newhart
Hi, Bob! by Joey Green (New York: St. Martin's Press, 1996)

The Chicago Fire
The Great Chicago Fire by David Lowe (New York: Dover, 1979)
Smoldering City by Karen Sawislak (Chicago: University of Chicago Press, 1995)
Mrs. O'Leary's Comet! by Mel Waskin (Chicago: Academy Chicago Publishers, 1985)

The Chicago River
The Chicago River by David M. Solzman (Chicago: Wild Onion Books, 1998)

The Haymarket Riot
Haymarket Revisited by William J. Adelman (Chicago: Illinois Labor History Society, 1986)

Pullman
Touring Pullman by William J. Adelman. (Chicago: Illinois Labor History Society, 1993)

The 1968 Democratic Convention Riots
Chicago '68 by David Farber (Chicago: University of Chicago Press, 1988)
Rights in Conflict by The Walker Commission (New York: Bantam Books, 1968)

Chicago Ghosts
Chicago Haunts, Revised Edition by Ursula Bielski (Chicago: Lake Claremont Press, 1998)
Chicagoland Ghosts by Dylan Clearfield (Grand Rapids, Mich.: Thunder Bay Press, 1997)

Graceland Cemetery
A Walk Through Graceland Cemetery by Barbara Lanctot (Chicago: Chicago Architecture Foundation, 1988)

2. Chicago Suburbs

Frances Willard and the WCTU

Frances Willard by Ruth Bordin (Chapel Hill, N.C.: University of North Carolina Press, 1986)

How I Learned to Ride the Bicycle by Frances E. Willard (Sunnyvale, Calif.: Fair Oaks Publishing Company, 1991)

Emma Goldman's Grave and the Haymarket Monument

Nature's Choicest Spot: A Guide to Forest Home and German Waldheim Cemeteries by The Historical Society of Oak Park and River Forest (Oak Park, Ill.: The Historical Society of Oak Park and River Forest, 1998)

Resurrection Mary

Resurrection Mary by Kenan Heise (Evanston, Ill.: Chicago Historical Bookworks, 1990)

Ernest Hemingway in Oak Park

Ernest Hemingway: The Oak Park Legacy edited by James Nagel (Tuscaloosa, Ala.: University of Alabama Press, 1996)

Bahá'í House of Worship

An Earthly Paradise by Julie Badiee (Oxford: George Ronald, 1992)

3. Northern Illinois

Mary Todd Lincoln

The Insanity Files by Mark E. Neeley, Jr. and R. Gerald McMurtry (Carbondale, Ill.: Southern Illinois Univesity Press, 1986)

Mary Todd Lincoln: A Biography by Jean H. Baker (New York: W. W. Norton, 1987)

Ronald Reagan

Innocents at Home by Garry Wills (New York: Doubleday, 1987)

Woodland Palace

Fred Francis and Woodland Palace by Rosemary Kuster (Henry, Ill.: Self-Published, 1975)

W. D. Boyce and the Boy Scouts

Boyce of Ottawa by John F. Sullivan (Ottawa, Ill.: Self-Published, 1985)

Billy Graham

Just As I Am by Billy Graham (San Francisco: HarperSanFrancisco, 1997)

Zion

Zion City, Illinois by Philip L. Cook (Syracuse, N.Y.: Syracuse University Press, 1996)

4. Central Illinois

Rockome Gardens
Rockome Sayings . . . and a Collection of Amusing Amish Dutch Expressions by
 Elvan Yoder (Arcola, Ill.: Rockome Gardens, n.d.)

Greenwood Cemetery
Where the Dead Walk by Troy Taylor (Forsyth, Ill.: Whitechapel Productions,
 1997)

Lincoln Tourism
In Lincoln's Footsteps by Don Davenport (Madison, Wisc.: Prairie Oak Press,
 1991)

The Mad Gasser of Mattoon
Rumor, Fear, and the Madness of Crowds by J. P. Chaplin (New York: Ballantine
 Books, 1959)

Route 66 in Illinois
Traveling the New, Historic Route 66 of Illinois by John Weiss (Frankfort: Ill.: A.O.
 Motivation Programs, 1997)

Abraham Lincoln's Tomb
The Tomb of Abraham Lincoln by Bess Martin (Springfield, Ill.: Lincoln Souvenir
 & Gift Shop, 1941)
The Great Abraham Lincoln Hijack by Bonnie Stahlman Speer (Norman, Okla.:
 Reliance Press, 1997)

5. Southern Illinois

The Piasa Bird
The Piasa by Ruth Means (Alton, Ill.: The Alton Council, Inc., n.d.)

Rev. Elijah Lovejoy
Freedom's Champion, Elijah Lovejoy by Paul Simon (Carbondale, Ill.: Southern
 Illinois University Press, 1994)

Our Lady of the Snows
National Shrine of Our Lady of the Snows by the Missionary Oblates of Mary
 Immaculate (Belleville, Ill.: National Shrine of Our Lady of the Snows, n.d.)

Charlie Birger
A Knight of Another Sort by Gary DeNeal (Carbondale, Ill.: Southern Illinois
 University Press, 1998)

Cahokia Mounds
The Ancient Splendor of Prehistoric Cahokia by Sidney Denny, Ernest Schusky,
 and John Adkins Richardson (Edwardsville, Ill.: Arressico, 1992)

Cleopatra's Tomb

The Mystery Cave of Many Faces by Russell Burrows and Fred Rydholm (Marquette, Mich.: Superior Heartland, 1991)

6. Theme Tours
Dead Circus Sideshow
Sideshow Folk (General)
Very Special People by Frederick Drimmer (New York: Citadel Press, 1991)
Robert Wadlow
Looking Back and Up by Sandra Hamilton (Alton, Ill.: Alton Museum of History and Art, 1996)
Museum of Science and Industry
Inventive Genius by Jay Pridmore (Chicago: Museum of Science and Industry, 1996)
Devil Baby of Hull House
Twenty Years at Hull House by Jane Addams (New York: MacMillan, 1910)

Mob Mania & Murder Mania
Chicago Crime (General)
The Wicked City by Curt Johnson (New York: Da Capo Press, 1998)
Chicago by Gaslight by Richard Lindberg (Chicago: Academy Chicago Publishers, 1996)
Al Capone
Al Capone by Rick Hornung (New York: Park Lane Press, 1998)
Mr. Capone by Robert J. Schoenberg (New York: Quill, 1992)
John Dillinger
Dillinger by G. Russell Girardin (Bloomington, Ind.: Indiana University Press, 1994)
Herman Mudgett and the Murder Castle
Depraved by Harold Schechter (New York: Pocket Books, 1994)
The Torture Doctor by David Franke (New York: Avon, 1975)
Richard Speck
The Crime of the Century by Dennis L. Breo and William J. Martin (New York: Bantam Books, 1993)
John Wayne Gacy
Buried Dreams by Tim Cahill (New York: Bantam, 1986)
The Man Who Killed Boys by Clifford L. Linedecker (New York: St. Martin's Paperbacks, 1980)

INDEX BY CITY NAME

Cairo
The Hewer (Halliday Park), 176
Carlock
Democrat Graveyard (Woodford County Cemetery), 141
Republican Graveyard (McLean County Cemetery), 141
Champaign
John Philip Sousa Library and Museum, 142
Charleston
World's Biggest Abe Lincoln, 143
Chester
Popeye Town, 177
Chicago
Buildings
  Amoco Building, 8
  Blackstone Hotel, 6
  Board of Trade Building, 11
  Chicago Cultural Center, 5
  Chicago Theater, 11
  Chicago Tribune Tower, 4
  Conrad Hilton, 6, 60
  First United Methodist Church, 11
  Hancock Tower, 9, 10, 68
  Harold Washington Chicago Public Library, 11
  Home Insurance Building, 2
  Inter-Continental Hotel, 11
  Jeweler's Building, 10
  Marina City, 10
  McCormick Building, 7
  Merchandise Mart, 11
  Metropolitan Correctional Center, 10
  Mies van der Rohe Skyscrapers, 11
  Murder Castle, 213
  North Avenue Beach House, 33
  Palmer House, 10–11
  Prudential Building, 8
  Reebie Storage and Moving, 36
  Sears Tower, 2–3, 6
  SelfPark, 3
  State of Illinois Building, 10
  311 S. Wacker Building, 6
  Water Tower, 10
  Wrigley Building, 11
  Wrigley Field, 14, 42, 67
Cemeteries
  Bohemian National Cemetery, 71
  Graceland Cemetery, 72–73
  Oak Woods Cemetery, 70–71

Graves, *cont.*
  Gacy, John Wayne (ashes), 218
  Lincoln Park, graves in, 69
  Nelson, Baby Face, 208
  Ruby, Jack, 210
  See also Chicago, Death Sites; Chicago, Murder
Homes
  The Christmas House, 38
  The Cross House / Mitch's Place, 34–35
  Palmer Mansion, 32–33
  Playboy Mansion, 37
  Raisin in the Sun House (Hansberry Home), 35
Loop, 2–11
Loop Tour Train, 5
Mob, 198–212
  Capone, Al, 198, 199–204
    Business, 199–200
    Grave (Mt. Carmel Cemetery), 203–4
    Home, 199–200
    Offices, 199–202
  Colosimo, Big Jim, 201
  Dillinger, John (*see* Chicago, Death Sites)
  Nelson, Baby Face (*see* Chicago, Death Sites)
  St. Valentine's Day Massacre, 202–203
  Untouchable Tours, 208–209
Monk Parakeets, 30–31
Murder
  Gacy, John Wayne, 217–18
  Hampton, Fred, (*see* Chicago, Death Sites, Black Panther Shoot-out)
  Leopold, Nathan, 214–15
  Leutgert, Adolph, 14
  Loeb, Richard, 214–15
  Murder Castle, 213
  Simpson, O.J. (Wyndam Garden Hotel), 219
  Speck, Richard, 215
  See also Chicago, Death Sites; Chicago, Graves; Chicago, Mob, Capone, Al
Museums
  American Gothic (Art Institute), 30
  American Police Center and Museum, 211–12
  Chicago Historical Society, 28–29
  Egyptian Gallery / Oriental Institute, 31
  Feet First Museum, 18
  Field Museum of Natural History, 31–32
  International Museum of Surgical Sciences and Hall of Immortals, 20
  Mexican Fine Arts Center, 77
  Museum of Broadcast Communications and Electronic Media, 19

Museums, *cont.*
  Museum of Holography, 22
  Museum of Science and Industry, 52–53, 193
  Radio Hall of Fame, 19
  Shedd Aquarium, 30
  Uncle Fun, 21–22
  The Uranus Telescope (Adler Planetarium), 30
Parks
  Grant Park, 7
  Lincoln Park, 60, 69
Public Art
  Big Ball and Pin (Woodmac Lanes), 23
  Big Weenies (Superdawg Drive-In), 24
  Buckingham Memorial Fountain, 26
  Deli-Sliced Duo, 193
  Eye Care Indian (Capitol Cigar Store), 25
  Hamburger Man (Pig Out Hot Dogs), 27
  Mr. Imagination's Grotto, 33
  Mussolini's Pillar / Balbo Monument, 23–24
  Nuclear Energy Statue, 27–28
  Pillar of Fire Monument, 49
  Pilsen Murals, 26
  Radium Gals Mosaic, 27
Rioting, 56–60
  Democratic National Convention of 1968, 60
  Haymarket Riot, 56–57, 89
  Police Riots, 60
Talk Shows, 46
Weeping Statues and Icons, 63–66
Collinsville
Cahokia Mounds, 178
World's Largest Catsup Bottle (Old Brooks Food Factory), 179–80
Dahinda
The Barn B&B, 147
Danville
Celebrity Way, 147–48
Darien
National Shrine of St. Therese Museum and Gift Shop (Carmelite Visitor's
  Center), 81–82
Decatur
Displaced Circus Animals (Decatur Chamber of Commerce), 192
Greenwood Cemetery, 150
Krekel's Kustard and the Chicken Cadillacs, 149
DeKalb
The Egyptian Theater, 115–16
Des Plaines
The Choo-Choo Restaurant, 83

Des Plaines, *cont.*
McDonald's #1 Store Museum, 82
Dixon
Ronald Reagan's Boyhood Home, 116–17
East Dundee
Santa's Village, 117
East Peoria
Twistee Treat Giant Cone, 151
Elmhurst
American Movie Palace Museum, 84
Lizzadro Museum of Lapidary Art, 85
Elsah
Mistake House (Principia College), 180
Evanston
Prehistoric Life Museum, 87–88
Rest Cottage and the WCTU Headquarters, 85–87
Forest Park
Emma Goldman's Grave (Forest Home Cemetery), 89
Haymarket Martyrs Monument, 89
Showman's Rest (Woodlawn Cemetery), 195–96
Galena
Belvedere Mansion, 118
Gays
Double-Decker Outhouse, 152
Hitler's Bicycle, 153
Hillside
Mt. Carmel Cemetery, 203–204
Justice
Resurrection Mary (Resurrection Cemetery), 90–91
Kewanee
Woodland Palace, 118–19
Lansing
First Lady Dolls (Lansing Historical Society and Museum), 91
Lemont
 Ghost Monks (St. James of the Sag Church), 92
Libertyville
Lamb's Farm Giant (Lamb's Farm), 119–20
Lincoln
Watermelon Statue, 153
Lincoln, Abraham, 144–46, 153, 162–63
Lincolnwood
Bunny Hutch, 93
Novelty Golf, 92
Makanda
Boomer's Grave (Railroad Depot), 181
Mattoon
The Mad Gasser (Matoon Chamber of Commerce), 154

McLean
Route 66 Hall of Fame Museum, 155
Metropolis
Superman's Hometown, 182–83
Midlothian
Bachelor's Grove Cemetery, 93–94
Monmouth
Wyatt Earp's Birthplace, 155–56
Morton Grove
Par King, 94
Mt. Caroll
Raven's Grin Inn, 120–21
Mt. Olive
Mother Jones's Grave, 184
Mt. Sterling
The World's Fattest (Dead) Man (Benville Cemetery), 196–97
Niles
Tower of Pisa, 95
Norway
Crashed Plane, 121
Norwood Park
John Wayne Gacy Murder Site, 217–18
Oak Brook
The Ray Kroc Museum, 96
Oak Park
(Ernest) Hemingway Birthplace and Museum, 97–98
(Frank Lloyd) Wright Studio and Museum, 97
Olney
White Squirrel Town, 185
Oquawka
Norma Jean the elephant Monument, 196
Oregon
Big Chief Black Hawk (Lowden State Park), 122
Ottawa
Effigy Tumuli, 122–23
Ottawa Scouting Museum, 123
Park Ridge
Museum of Anesthesiology–Wood Library, 99
Quincy
Hee Haw Pickup, 158
Jesus in a Tree (Calvary Cemetery), 156–57
Lincoln-Douglas Valentine Museum, 159
Villa Katharine, 157–58
Rantoul
Octave Chanute Aerospace Museum, 159–60
River Grove
Baby Face Nelson Grave (St. Joseph's Cemetery), 208

INDEX BY SITE NAME

Prehistoric Life Museum (Dave's Down to Earth Rock Shop), 87–88
Prudential Building, 8
Radio Hall of Fame, 19
Radium Gals Mosaic (Navy Pier), 27
Raisin in the Sun House (Hansberry Home), 35
Raven's Grin Inn, 120–21
The Ray Kroc Museum, 96
Reagan, Ronald, boyhood home of, 116–17
Reebie Storage and Museum, 36
Republican Graveyard (McLean County Cemetery), 141
Rest Cottage and the WCTU Headquarters, 85–87
Resthaven Cemetery, 76
Resurrection Mary (Resurrection Cemetery), 90–91
Reverend Lovejoy Monument (Alton City Cemetery), 171
Rockome Gardens, 136–37
Rosehill Cemetery, 74–75
Route 66 Hall of Fame Museum (Dixie Trucker's Home), 155
Ruby, Jack, grave of, 210
Santa's Village, 117
Sears Tower, 2–3, 6
SelfPark, 3
Shedd Aquarium, 30
Shiloh House / Zion Historical Society, 130–31
Showman's Rest , 195–96
Simpson, O.J. (Wyndam Garden Hotel), 219
Speck, Richard, 215
The State of Illinois Building, 10
Stickney Mansion, 114–15
St. Johannes Cemetery, 76
St. Valentine's Day Massacre, 202–203
Submarines, 52–53
Sue, the *T. rex* fossil, 32
Superman's Hometown, 182–83
Talk Shows in Chicago, 46
Tomb for Accordions (Oak Ridge Cemetery), 163
Tower of Pisa, 95
Twistee Treat Giant Cone, 151
Uncle Fun, 21–22
Union Stockyards, 12, 13
Unshackled! (Pacific Garden Mission), 62
Untouchable Tours, 208–209
The Uranus Telescope (Adler Planetarium), 30
Villa Katherine, 157–58
Virgin Mary, apparitions of, 63–66, 172
Wacker Building, 6
The Wall of Turin, 66
Watermelon Statue, 153